The Character Blueprint

Crafting Effective Teams Through Personal Development

Tommy Brooks

ISBN: 979-8-89979-608-1

Dedication

For the quiet strugglers, the unseen fighters, and the resilient souls whose strength is rarely recognized but deeply felt. To those whose perseverance isn't celebrated in headlines yet shapes the character of those around them—this is for you. May this book remind us all that real leadership is rooted in empathy, and true character is forged through adversity. You are the silent architects of a better world.

Acknowledgment

Writing this book has been a humbling and rewarding journey—one I could not have completed without the unwavering support of so many remarkable individuals.

To my wife and daughter: your patience, encouragement, and belief in me—even during moments of doubt—gave me the strength to keep moving forward. You are my foundation, and I'm endlessly grateful.

To my mentors and colleagues, your insights, wisdom, and honest feedback shaped this book far beyond my expectations. A special thank you to "The Chief," whose guidance helped sharpen my thinking and expand my understanding of authentic leadership. Your influence will forever echo through these pages.

And to you, the reader—thank you for walking this journey with me. May *The Character Blueprint* become a mirror, a compass, and a companion on your own path of growth.

With deep gratitude,

Tommy Brooks

About the Author

After dedicating an impressive 23 years of his life to the United States Navy, Tommy Brooks recognized the potential to use his extensive experience to make a positive impact on individuals seeking to develop and improve their leadership skills. This realization led him to embark on the journey of writing *The Character Blueprint: Crafting Effective Teams Through Personal Development.*

Throughout his tenure in the Navy, Tommy led numerous highly skilled teams operating some of the most sophisticated warships in the world. During this time, he gained a deep understanding of the importance of well-developed leadership skills—not just in military settings, but also in everyday life. However, the command attributes that proved the most powerful might surprise some, especially originating in the armed forces.

Mentoring and training many talented and courageous military personnel allowed Tommy to demonstrate a comprehensive skill set. He earned certifications as a Navy Leadership Development Facilitator, Classroom Instructor, and Master Training Specialist. Contributing to the development of brilliant minds shaping today's naval leaders was one of the greatest honors of his life. His ultimate goal is to transform exceptional individuals into exemplary leaders in the civilian community, whenever the opportunity arises.

The views expressed in this publication are those of the author and do not necessarily reflect the official policy or position of the Department of Defense or the U.S. government. The public release clearance of this publication by the Department of Defense does not imply Department of Defense endorsement or factual accuracy of the material.

Preface

Character is the foundation of exceptional leadership. Whether in our personal lives or professional endeavors, the qualities that define us often determine the impact we have on those around us. This book is a guide to understanding and cultivating the traits that foster personal growth and create effective teams.

Imagine meeting someone who radiates authenticity and compassion. Their presence inspires trust, motivates action, and encourages collaboration. Such individuals often seem exceptional—but their character and leadership skills are not innate; they are developed over time through intentional effort.

The *Character Blueprint* combines practical advice, real-life experiences, and proven strategies to help readers embark on their own journeys of personal development. By strengthening character, we empower ourselves and those we lead, building a better future together.

Join me as we explore the principles, some surprising, that lead to real strength and resilience. *The Character Blueprint* can help anyone with an open mind and teachable spirit discover how they can transform not only their own life but also the teams and communities they serve.

Contents

Dedication i
Acknowledgment ii
About the Author ii
Preface v
Chapter 1: Introduction 1
Chapter 2: Understanding Character's Impact on Team and Business 19
Chapter 3: Self-reflection and Character Assessment 29
Chapter 4: Integrity as the Cornerstone of Character 47
Chapter 5: Developing Emotional Intelligence for Effective Collaboration 58
Chapter 6: Cultivating Resilience and Adaptability 68
Chapter 7: Building a Culture of Collaboration and Accountability 81
Chapter 8: Conflict Resolution and Effective Problem-solving..... 94
Chapter 9: Leading with Character 107
Chapter 10: Nurturing Presence and Participation 124
Chapter 11: Sustaining Character Growth in Teams and Organizations 137
Chapter 12: A Call to Action 152

Chapter 1: Introduction

Imagine being in a room filled with people. One person stands out above all others, not because of their physical appearance or achievements, but because of their exceptional personal character. The atmosphere in the room seems to shift when this individual enters—they command attention without saying a word.

As they make their way through the crowd, heads turn, and conversations fade. It isn't their stature that makes them stand out, but the aura of integrity, warmth, and compassion radiating from their being. People can't help but be drawn to their presence, feeling an immediate sense of trust and admiration.

As the room gradually settles into silence, this person's actions speak louder than any words they might utter. They move with purpose and grace, effortlessly navigating through the sea of hushed human beings. With each interaction, they display genuine interest in others, taking the time to listen attentively and offer words of encouragement or support.

This person's humility is striking. Rather than seeking attention or recognition for themselves, they consistently lift others up. Whether it is a simple compliment, a kind gesture, or a willingness to lend a helping hand, their actions demonstrate a deep understanding of the power derived from investing in others.

In this room full of people, the atmosphere seems to transform. The air becomes charged with inspiration and motivation as this individual's positive energy permeates every corner. Others in the room begin to emulate their behavior, following their lead. Consideration and empathy spread like a warm blanket throughout the space.

Beyond their words and actions, this person stands out because of the consistency and authenticity of their character. They embody their values in every tone, facial expression, and motion their body language speaks. Their mere presence has a profound impact on everyone around them. This person is a walking blueprint for character and exceptional leadership. And though it might surprise others, they were not born this way, their leadership mastery is a learned behavior.

We know there is no defined toolset that must be followed, like a cookie-cutter system, for someone to succeed in life. Each person follows their own pace and their own goals in their own way to achieve what they desire. Contrary to what some might think, an individual's success is not defined by how far ahead they are in front of everyone else.

However, a particular trait makes a person stand out in a crowd. It is a thing called character. The way people rummage through life, the choices they make, their beliefs, and what they do, all of this defines the makeup of human beings. The words of Billy Graham emphasize character as the most essential building block in any person's life.

"When wealth is lost, nothing is lost; when health is lost, something is lost; when character is lost, all is lost."

-Billy Graham

Some terms used to describe character include integrity, moral strength, resolve, firmness of purpose, and fortitude. In essence, it is the certain aspect a person abides by, regardless of their environment or circumstances. Character defines the behavior and performance of a person—it is *why* they do what they do.

The way a person lives is defined by the set of character traits the person commits to following. Some people might say character is natural, simply a part of the genetic package we're handed, like our eye and hair color. While it is known that a person's character is established and changed throughout different phases of their life, character is also something a person adapts to in response to what happens around them or to them.

Where does a person learn to be honest, brave, and emotionally strong? This is not something you are simply born with. Instead, these kinds of attributes are developed through early influences, as well as your actions as you embark on different life experiences.

Surrounding yourself with positive influences is vital. The hands of appropriate authoritative figures can mold a person into something good. Thus, you need an ongoing influence that induces some positivity within you, so you have a chance at the best possible outcome.

How is the Character of a Person Defined?

How a person makes their choices is dependent on their character, and that mentality is based on different factors. A person's character is weighted by the basic elements of values, morals, and beliefs.

Values

Every human being alive follows their own set of values. These determinations are fed into a person as a core belief.

If a person's core value is kindness, they don't mind being kind to others, even on the hardest of days. If dependability is a priority value, then showing up, with a "no excuses" attitude will be the internal rudder that guides whether promises are kept. If adaptability is an important value, then making modifications for others will not require much energy or sacrifice. Values are typically something that drives a person's actions without any conscious thought process.

Morals

Using their moral standard as a filter, a person determines their behaviors.

Morals are simple, basic rules that a person resolves to follow to become a "better" or more virtuous person. Morals are based on an individual's perceptions. Morals can include commitments to values such as honesty, consideration, and loyalty. When a person exhibits questionable character, their moral compass may not align with the outcomes they desire and can be a result of many complex factors, including significant trauma.

Adherence to one's moral principles influences their performance, whether at work or at home. When challenges arise, it's valuable to reflect on how our morals shape our decisions, to better understand our own actions. This introspection allows us to determine if adjusting our standards of acceptability is necessary to enact positive changes in our behavior and mindset, leading to improved results.

Belief

A belief is something a person considers to be true, and each person's set of beliefs is exceptionally unique.

Belief drives a person's assumption that something is wrong or right. It can vary from person to person. It doesn't necessarily mean that something true to one person is true to another. An example of different beliefs in society is that of different religions. The mere difference in belief system shapes perception, decisions made, actions taken, and ultimately, how a person views that life turns out for them.

The combination of values, morals, and beliefs also make up the character of a person. Based on the formula of these three elements, the character of a person varies.

Now that we've covered the basic definition of character, let's take it a step further. What dictates a *good* character? Here's your answer: A person's virtues define his or her good character. Moreover, all factors, including behavior, body language, and communication skills, reflect a person's character type.

Based on someone's virtues, certain character traits help assess the scale between good and bad. Nevertheless, evaluating a person's character is not exactly black and white.

A person could have what are perceived as bad traits that don't exactly taint their character. For example, indecisiveness might mean a person has difficulty making decisions or committing to choices and can delay progress or create frustration but this doesn't reflect poorly on a person's core values. Also, a person's difficulty in delegating or assigning tasks to others might lead to burnout or inefficiency without impacting one's core values or abilities. However, there are certain traits that can better highlight a person's nature.

Character Traits

Each human being's personality is revealed through different types of traits, including strengths and weaknesses. Examples of character traits include:

Leadership

The cliché "No person is born a leader. Leaders are made through life experiences such as overcoming adversity, professional training, or intentional pursuit," reflects a widely held belief about leadership development. This suggests that leadership is not an inherent trait one is born with but rather a skill and quality that develops over time. While some individuals may have natural inclinations or aptitudes that make leadership easier for them, leadership itself is shaped by experiences and choices rather than being a preordained characteristic.

Facing and overcoming difficulties can develop resilience, problem-solving skills, and empathy, if you allow it. Adversity often tests and refines one's character, helping individuals learn how to lead others through tough times. Experiencing setbacks and failures teaches important lessons about perseverance, humility, and adapting strategies, all of which are crucial leadership qualities.

Formal education, workshops, seminars, and on-the-job training equip individuals with leadership skills such as communication, decision-making, and strategic thinking. Learning from experienced leaders and receiving constructive feedback helps individuals understand leadership principles in the trenches and how to apply them effectively.

Actively seeking opportunities for growth, such as pursuing leadership roles, taking on challenging projects, or engaging in personal development activities such as reading books, watching educational videos, taking online courses, or listening to podcasts on the subject demonstrate commitment to becoming a better leader. Leaders often have a clear vision and set specific goals for their development. Intentional pursuit involves setting goals and working diligently toward them, refining leadership skills along the way.

The idea that leaders are made rather than born emphasizes that leadership is a dynamic and evolving skill set. It highlights the importance of personal development, experiential learning, and intentional effort. By embracing challenges, seeking continuous improvement, and learning from experiences, individuals can cultivate the qualities and skills needed to lead others successfully. *The Character Blueprint* is structured with foundational elements every good leader needs to build on.

Integrity

Integrity is the commitment to upholding virtuous core beliefs. It involves enduring and not yielding to conformity pressures in the presence of adversity or challenging situations.

A person with integrity is someone who is not easily fazed by disturbing events, though they often must choose to grip their integrity time and time again. With their strong willpower and belief, they consider themselves able to overcome any situation in life. It is one of the strongest character traits that makes leaders shine in any personal or professional setting. And integrity can be learned through ongoing education, reframing thoughts, speaking affirmations, and spending time with people who consistently work and live by this philosophy.

Honesty

Honesty is a fundamental virtue that resonates with the idea that truthfulness serves as a cornerstone for every decision. Embracing honesty can lead to a more authentic and non-toxic lifestyle.

Dishonesty, including withholding the truth, can significantly impact how others perceive an individual. Regardless of the reasons behind lying, deceptive acts are generally seen as undermining trust.

Having an honest virtue shapes your character into something robust. Honesty is not only critical with everyone around you, but you also owe absolute truth to yourself most of all. In terms of business leadership, honest self-analysis provides constructive criticism so you can identify areas for improvement, set realistic goals, and strive for professional excellence.

Humility

Being humble and modest is an essential key to unlocking any door. No matter how far you have come in your life, don't forget where you started. Leaders who conduct themselves as servants devoted to the greater good, who remember their own humble beginnings, rarely fall on the sword of their own arrogance.

A person who is kind and modest despite a higher position or status among the group of people they are leading is the one who stands out and rises. Leading with strength means lowering yourself when necessary to meet a person where they are.

Empathy

It is vital and the most humane form of leadership to stay open to other people's feelings. Knowing how to deal with emotions and not discard them is another basic requirement for exceptional leaders.

Empathy leads to a lasting connection between people, which is important in any professional setting. Regarding other people as human beings with feelings instead of treating them like inanimate objects is a way to promote a healthy emotional environment and productive working conditions. Many effective leaders understand the power of offering an appropriate hug to demonstrate support, compassion, or care. As a naval officer, I have certainly provided a shoulder to those I've led when a situation called for it—many times.

Importance of Character in Different Aspects of Life

The existence of good character backs the prospect of a healthy and happy personal and professional life. The character of a person defines their aura, and their aura represents the positive or negative energy they radiate. How they perceive their life situations and how they react to them determines the type of character they emit.

There are two types of settings where the character of a person is evaluated:

Personal Life

A person's character shapes his or her relationship with those around them. Every connection is built on these blocks:

- Honesty
- Empathy
- Loyalty

Consider a person who is consistently dishonest with their partner, child, friend, co-worker, vendor, or customer. At the end of the day, people will begin questioning every statement, explanation, or story they tell. Dishonesty triggers resentment, leading to an inability to maintain strong, healthy bonds.

A person who does not show empathy for people demonstrates a lack of concern for others, which is seen as a self-centered approach. Few, if any of us, wish to waste time and energy spent in the presence of those who care only for themselves.

Certainly, a disloyal person is not appreciated in any circumstance. Feeling as if the next betrayal could happen at any moment or wondering when another backstabbing will occur does not lead to healthy connections.

But before we jump to conclusions about those we believe are missing the character blocks of honesty, empathy, and loyalty, we must make one consideration. Often, situations and people are not what they first appear to be.

Imagine if people etched labels on the foreheads of others that describe the assumed qualities they see without delving deeper to determine accuracy or why. While the idea of labeled qualities might seem convenient, the complexity of human nature and the richness of interpersonal relationships ultimately benefits from a more holistic and open-minded approach. Seeking to understand others and listening to learn leads to more successful outcomes.

Professional Life

Professional environments differ greatly from personal life for many leaders. Some people who feel the pressures of responsibility tend to put on masks at work and attend to the professional world wearing a persona. But pretending only gets us so far. If illusion is one of your character traits, it ends up defining your work ethic and leads to exhaustion when the mask gets too heavy. And the weight of illusion catches up with everyone.

Success in a professional environment involves more than just individual skills or tasks; it requires effective interpersonal dynamics to foster a positive and productive work atmosphere. Interacting with diverse individuals requires a collaborative mindset, open and clear communication, and a balanced and optimistic outlook. You cannot successfully fit into a surrounding without cooperating with other people. Maintaining a working relationship with colleagues where competition is a factor can be tricky if you do not have an established set of rules to follow.

How you approach those who work alongside you significantly influences your professional results. Key aspects to consider include:

- Ethics
- Commitment
- Improvement
- Time management

Adhering to a disciplined work routine, efficiently managing time, delivering positive results, and more importantly, using constructive criticism to improve your skills, all contribute to one's character in a professional environment.

Benefits of Excellent Individual Character

The success of any team, any great organization, or a growing business is dependent on each individual's excellence.

Just as a game of football relies on the outstanding skills and character of each player for overall team wins, an organization or business thrives when composed of individuals with excellent character. In football, the synergy of a team is built upon the commitment, discipline, and proficiency of each player, along with the guidance of an effective coach. Success hinges on the collective performance of all.

Similarly, within an organization, the ethical conduct, dedication, and competence of individual members contribute to a cohesive and high-performing team. A group with members possessing excellent character traits such as accountability and collaboration, fuels a trustworthy work culture. This basis better equips people to tackle challenges, ultimately resulting in overall victory for the organization. A leader who sets the tone first by example and second through training emphasis creates success-driven expectations that generate profits and a more pleasant workplace.

Each person sees the world differently from others, evidenced by their habits, choices, and behaviors. However, when working in a team for a collective goal, some individual traits require alterations to fit in better for a greater purpose. Thus, collective achievement leads to individual success.

In a business setting, certain individual characteristics are especially important.

Disciplined Work Ethic

Every person has a set of rules and guidelines they follow. Staying true to those rules while polishing a supportive work attitude cultivates individual greatness—this is called discipline.

A person with a strong sense of discipline contributes to the promotion of efficient workflow and effective management.

As each individual embraces their own disciplined approach, it collectively establishes a work environment characterized by both self-motivation and ethics.

Creative Outcome

In every professional setting, creative thinking and innovative approaches are essential. Having a unique and exceptional set of skills enables individuals to introduce ideas that can significantly impact various aspects of an organization.

Consider the invention of the dishwasher. Someone dared to let their mind wander freely, generating an idea that, with the support and collaboration of others, became a tangible reality.

Adaptability

In any business, there are often unexpected circumstances that need to be dealt with immediately. The ability to adapt to any situation is crucial in workplace leadership.

Showing adaptability to any overwhelming or adverse situation contributes to the success in a business.

While one's upbringing influences principles and morals, it's important for leaders to know that these aspects should be open to change, if facts prove relevant. The willingness to learn and improve oneself promotes overall well-being.

With guidance and self-discovery, one can refine one's viewpoints and skills, leading to enhancements in every aspect of life. A leader can also help open eyes, ears, and minds for those they are responsible for, to see evidence otherwise missed, lending to expanded views and greater adaptability.

One might ask, who am I to help modify the way someone sees their own life story? In my case, I have interacted with many people, and through them, I have gathered various pieces of information and been on the receiving end of numerous influences. Moreover, many of these experiences have helped me learn how to improve my character, become a better leader, and ignite the same spark among others. I believe much of what I've learned needs to be heard by others.

I have discovered multiple traits crucial to developing the capability for resilience in every situation. Through my time in the Naval services, I learned the importance of self-awareness and clear communication.

Next, I will share a couple of brief stories about my experience with two vastly different leaders. As a retired Navy man, I call them, *Insights from an Old Salt.* (Yes, I am the Old Salt.) Believing there's nothing like a good narrative to highlight a point, I will also provide *Insights from an Old Salt* at the end of subsequent chapters. But now, let me tell you about those leaders.

Insights from An Old Salt

I vividly recall a challenging moment during a naval training exercise where a senior leader, whom we all respected deeply, demonstrated a lack of self-awareness and communication ability. As we navigated through a complex series of maneuvers, it became evident that there were significant gaps in our understanding of the mission objectives. Despite our concerns and attempts to seek clarification, our leader remained steadfast in their belief that everything was proceeding according to plan, dismissing our questions and feedback without consideration.

As the exercise progressed, it became increasingly clear that the leader's lack of self-awareness hindered our ability to execute the mission effectively. Miscommunications and misunderstandings arose, leading to confusion and frustration among the team. Despite our best efforts to adapt and overcome our challenges, the leader's inability to recognize their limitations prevented us from achieving our full potential.

In hindsight, this memory serves as a reminder of the importance of self-awareness, self-understanding, and effective communication in leadership. It highlights the profound impact that a leader's blind spots can have on their team and the mission at hand. It also emphasizes the necessity for leaders to continually reflect on their actions, seek feedback from others, and remain open to self-improvement so they can lead with clarity, authenticity, and effectiveness.

In contradiction to that experience, there was a time when a reputable commanding officer was responsible for our naval exercises. I always heard he was a man of great character. I never got the gist of it until he led our team through a series of challenging exercises. He was a remarkable man. Starting on day one, he made the mission clear to us, acknowledged its complexity, and presented us with ways to navigate difficult tasks. Through communication and his own self-awareness, he helped us overcome our mental barriers and work for the goal passionately.

In the face of uncertainty, the commander's willingness to confront his own limitations and seek input from others proved to be a game-changer. By facilitating a culture of trust and collaboration, he empowered each member of the team to contribute their unique perspectives and insights. Through candid discussions and collective problem-solving, we were able to adapt our strategies and overcome the challenges we faced with resilience and unity.

From that moment on, I learned the importance of building life around strong character traits. Because at the end of the day, it is robust character that stands out among a crowd of people.

As we look deeper into *The Character Blueprint*, we'll delve into profound ways to impact the growth of your team and business by enhancing individual efforts. So, grab a comfortable seat, maybe a cup of coffee, and let's explore the transformative power of personal development.

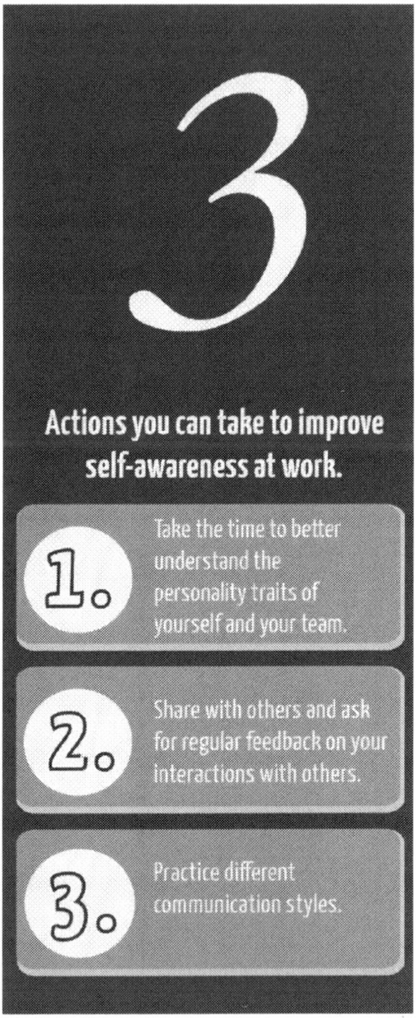
3
Actions you can take to improve self-awareness at work.
1.
Take the time to better understand the personality traits of yourself and your team.
2.
Share with others and ask for regular feedback on your interactions with others.
3.
Practice different communication styles.

Chapter 2: Understanding Character's Impact on Team and Business

An individual's character shapes their journey through life, with each trait manifesting through their decisions and actions. Particularly in professional contexts, one's character stands out as the foremost defining factor.

When an individual within a team displays dishonesty and disloyalty, it invariably leads to diminished work efficiency and quality. A lack of trust results in a hindered work environment.

Adherence to ethics and etiquette is imperative in reputable workplaces. Deviating from these standards not only dampens the collective spirit but also creates toxicity, making it challenging for companies to retain valuable employees.

Individuals naturally seek environments conducive to productivity and personal fulfillment, particularly in professional settings where motivation and effectiveness are crucial. Without such an environment, performance suffers, and the business incurs losses in terms of quality *and* quantity produced.

The foundation of a healthy work environment lies in the integrity of each individual's character. Compromising this virtue adversely impacts the overall dynamics of the business setting and teamwork.

Certain personal traits significantly influence an individual's contribution to teamwork and overall business performance.

Recognizing and understanding these traits is essential for business success.

In any thriving organization, effective teamwork is paramount. Successfully navigating diverse backgrounds and mindsets within a team is a challenge worth mastering. Despite inevitable disagreements or differing interpretations of rules, the ability to align one's mindset with others' for the mutual benefit of the business is what ultimately matters.

Character's Impact on Teamwork and Business

The size of a project team significantly influences its outcomes. For instance, imagine a scenario where only six individuals are assigned to build a bridge—it's clearly not an optimal allocation of resources. Just as the number of team members impacts a project, so does the quality, which is closely tied to the personalities and character of each individual involved.

You might question the relevance of character in this context. However, certain traits are fundamental prerequisites for effective teamwork, underscoring the importance of individual character in collaborative settings.

Effective communication is essential for establishing strong relationships. When communication falters, misunderstandings arise, leading to confusion and discord. Whether within personal relationships or among team members working toward a common goal, clear communication is key. Without articulating needs and expectations, achieving optimal outcomes becomes challenging. Moreover, the manner and tone of communication significantly impact its effectiveness. Respectful communication is paramount, as it ensures that messages are received and understood positively, fostering trust and collaboration. In essence, words spoken with respect are the ones that truly resonate and contribute to successful endeavors.

Trust is the cornerstone of any meaningful connection. Without it, relationships crumble like buildings lacking a solid foundation, prone to weakened collapse. When trust is absent, chaos ensues, leaving behind a disarray of broken bonds and shattered expectations.

Trusting one's colleagues to fulfill their designated roles is essential. Merely assigning tasks without confidence in their ability to execute undermines both their competence and the integrity of the relationship. Empowering others with trust encourages their growth and strengthens the bonds of collaboration and mutual reliance.

It's crucial for individuals to support the integrity and efforts of their colleagues. This mutual backing not only nurtures motivation and confidence within the team but also opens doors to new possibilities. Knowing that peers are supportive is encouraging when taking risks and embarking on innovative ventures. With the assurance that others have their back, individuals feel more empowered to strive for greatness. This extra push and boost in confidence often proves to be the catalyst for achieving remarkable feats.

Accountability, often overlooked, is a vital character trait that deserves more recognition. Failing to take responsibility for one's actions can breed distrust and weaken the foundation of professional relationships, potentially leading to the breakdown of the working relationship.

Regardless of the tasks at hand, individuals must consistently demonstrate accountability. Avoiding responsibility or resorting to dishonesty only exacerbates problems, undermining trust and integrity. It's imperative for individuals to confront their actions openly and truthfully, reinforcing trust and strengthening professional bonds.

Teamwork's Importance in Business Success

The significance of teamwork in achieving business success can be likened to completing a puzzle. Just as unconnected puzzle pieces create chaos, even a single misplaced piece can render the entire picture incomplete. This analogy stresses the importance of individual contributions within a team and their collective impact on overall business success.

Several factors related to teamwork are instrumental in determining results. *The Character Blueprint* is designed with this in mind.

By leveraging the contrasting knowledge and skill sets of team members, businesses can enhance productivity and efficiency through expanded wisdom. Drawing upon each individual's strengths leads to increased output and more streamlined processes.

A cohesive and goal-oriented team stimulates an environment where creativity thrives. When team members are encouraged to take risks and are supported by their peers, they can explore innovative ideas and concepts. This ultimately enhances business outcomes by utilizing fresh approaches.

Teamwork also presents opportunities for both personal and professional growth among individuals. Working alongside people with varied experiences allows team members to learn from each other's expertise, contributing to their development and expanding their skill sets.

The risk of burnout is reduced when team members feel supported and appreciated. Encouragement from colleagues, combined with constructive feedback and recognition, creates a sense of belonging and reduces the likelihood of physical and emotional exhaustion, thereby sustaining productivity.

The importance of individual character cannot be overstated in the success of a team's effort. Strong individual character translates into effective teamwork, which in turn drives organizational success. Understanding the compatibility between individual character and team dynamics highlights the significant contribution each person makes.

In large organizations comprised of thousands of individuals segmented into numerous teams, it's easy to feel insignificant. However, each person's input matters significantly, akin to a droplet adding weight to the ocean. That massive amount of water would not exist were it not for many singular drops pooled together.

Recognizing this dynamic emphasizes that every individual is valued, and their insights hold importance in every task undertaken by the organization.

"The strength of the team is each member. The strength of each member is the team."

-Phil Jackson

The quote above speaks directly to the concept of individual contribution within a team, emphasizing that the strength of the whole is inherently linked to the strength of its members and vice versa. This concept sets the stage for exploring how a person's character not only influences themselves but also impacts the overall group potency.

The foundation of organizational success lies in effective teamwork, as evidenced by a study conducted by Hoegl and Gemuenden (2001), which found that exceptional organizational success hinges on successful team performance. The study highlighted honesty as a fundamental character trait that fosters high-quality teamwork and organizational achievement.

Additionally, research by Van Woerkam (2020) established a model emphasizing the importance of harnessing individual strengths. It revealed that optimal team and organizational performance stem from effectively leveraging the diverse strengths of each team member, with individual and team success being closely intertwined.

A well-performing team creates an environment where individuals can approach their work creatively, finding enjoyment in their tasks rather than viewing them as mere obligations. This insight, supported by Philippe Dubreuil's findings in *The Journal of Positive Psychology*, stresses how a healthy team dynamic enhances individual productivity.

Moreover, the true strength of teamwork lies in assembling a diverse range of individuals with varying strengths rather than similar skill sets. This diversity fosters efficiency and innovation within the team, as each member brings unique perspectives and capabilities to the table.

The key to achieving both team and individual success lies in a structured approach:

- Strength Awareness: Identifying individual strengths
- Credibility: Trusting and relying on these strengths
- Coordination: Assigning roles based on these strengths

By diligently working toward a common goal and leveraging the strengths of each team member, both teamwork and individual performance are enhanced. A symbiotic relationship emerges where a well-performing team inspires individual growth, ultimately leading the organization to success.

"The character of a man is the result of two things: heredity and environment. But heredity is the less important of the two."

-Dwight L. Moody.

In essence, the words above highlight the pivotal role of individual character in shaping success. They reaffirm this chapter's central theme that the character traits of each person significantly contribute to the collective outcome within a group setting.

Insights from An Old Salt

As a young submariner, I experienced an event that emphasized the critical importance of communication and trust in our high-pressure environment.

It was a routine day at sea. The steady hum of the turbine's rotation merged seamlessly with the sharp hiss of steam, creating a harmonious purr that embodied the raw power and efficiency of the machinery that moved us forward.

As the overhead lights flickered within the confines of the submarine, a sense of purpose and camaraderie filled the air. Little did we know, our team, comprised of engineers and technicians, was about to be tested. Suddenly, a series of alarms pierced the silence, signaling a malfunction in the propulsion system. Panic threatened to engulf us.

Without hesitation, our team sprang into action. Every member of the engineering team swiftly and effectively relayed information. We assessed the situation, shared insights and troubleshooting techniques, and offered support where we could. Each member's expertise and dedication, combined with clear and concise communication, allowed us to quickly identify and correct the issue. There were no egos or hidden agendas in that moment of heightened emotions—only a shared commitment to the safety and success of our mission.

Through perseverance and teamwork, we emerged victorious. Problem solved.

The engine room hummed to life once more, the rhythmic whirl of the machinery serving as a testament to our aligned fortitude. When we all gathered for debriefing, there was a palpable sense of pride and mutual respect that filled the air. We had faced a daunting challenge head-on and emerged stronger than ever, united by the unwavering trust that bound us together.

Building Trust Through Connection

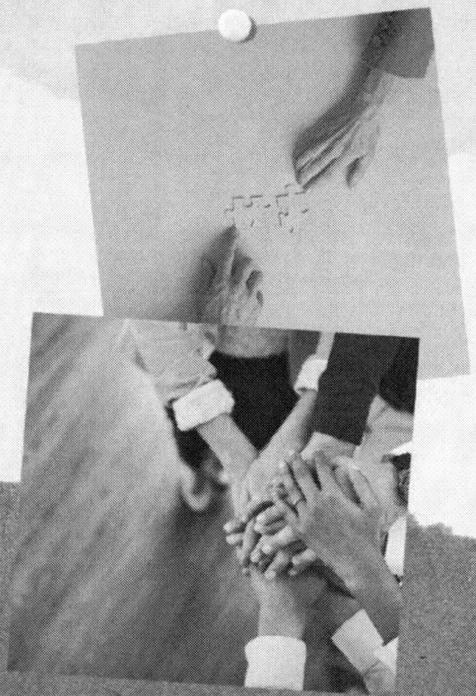

Support, accountability, and open communication are essential.

Chapter 3: Self-reflection and Character Assessment

Consistently monitoring and regulating one's character traits is necessary for ongoing personal growth. Engaging in regular self-reflection is a powerful tool for identifying areas of improvement, understanding one's strengths and weaknesses, and maintaining alignment with personal values. It allows individuals to recognize patterns in behavior, thoughts, and emotions that might hinder progress. Through self-reflection, a person can develop greater self-awareness, which is crucial for making intentional changes that promote growth.

In addition, regularly evaluating one's actions and decisions helps ensure they are consistent with long-term goals, and helps a person stay on track. This practice not only supports personal development but also builds emotional intelligence, resilience, and a more compassionate approach to interactions with others.

Ultimately, self-reflection initiates a mindset of lifelong learning, where individuals remain open to feedback, are willing to adapt, and continuously strive to evolve their character in ways that enhance both their personal and professional lives.

"Knowing yourself is the beginning of all wisdom."

-Aristotle, Metaphysics (350 BC).

In his book, *Metaphysics*, ancient Greek philosopher, Aristotle, stressed the importance of discovering yourself. He believed that self-awareness is key to gaining wisdom. When we understand our strengths, shortcomings, what matters to us, and what we want, we can make better choices and live a life true to ourselves. This reminds us to actively explore who we are–our beliefs, values, and why we do what we do–and to keep striving to learn more about ourselves.

There is a lot a person can unearth through self-reflection. It helps an individual discover hidden or overlooked attributes due to the busyness of everyday life or habitual thinking patterns. By taking time to pause and examine one's thoughts, feelings, and behaviors, individuals can uncover underlying motivations, biases, and beliefs that may influence their actions.

Self-reflection also provides an opportunity to recognize subconscious habits that might not align with personal values or goals. Identifying conflicts within ourselves can explain why we sometimes undermine our own desires or efforts. Newfound awareness can lead to a deeper understanding of certain behavior patterns, as well as areas where growth is needed. Additionally, it can reveal strengths that might have gone unrecognized, empowering individuals to discover abilities that bring them deeper satisfaction and greater joy.

In this way, self-reflection acts as a mirror, helping individuals gain clarity about who they truly are and what they aspire to become, ultimately contributing to greater authenticity and personal fulfilment.

Self-reflection plays a crucial role in understanding how others might perceive you. With deeper insights, you can better communicate how you prefer to be approached and understood. Often, problems arise not from a particular issue, but from how we interpret or perceive it. The way a message is delivered and received greatly influences our understanding of its true meaning. For instance, someone may intend to be helpful in their communication, but if their tone is off-putting, it can create a negative impression. When something deviates from our usual expectations or standards, it often explains why we react negatively. Recognizing this can help us respond more thoughtfully and adjust our perceptions to avoid unnecessary conflict.

Self-reflection allows you to pause and take a deeper look at your thoughts, actions, and experiences, helping you identify patterns that either support or hinder your personal growth. Through self-reflection, you can gain a clearer understanding of your values, goals, and the underlying motivations behind your actions. This awareness gives you the opportunity to make conscious decisions about how to change, adapt, or enhance aspects of your life that need improvement.

Moreover, self-reflection helps you build emotional intelligence by encouraging you to assess how your feelings influence your reactions and interactions with others. This process of introspection allows you to better manage your emotions, communicate more effectively, and respond to challenges with greater resilience and patience.

Ultimately, self-reflection generates a sense of accountability, as it pushes you to take ownership of your growth and development. By regularly engaging in the practice of assessing the *why* behind what you do, you create a foundation for continuous self-improvement, leading to a more authentic, balanced, and fulfilling life.

When individuals possess a heightened sense of self-awareness, they become more conscientious regarding their personal growth trajectory. They engage in introspection to assess not only their emotional development but also the overall trajectory of their lives. This includes evaluating whether they are experiencing meaningful growth or if they are stagnating and remaining static in their journey. They recognize the importance of actively monitoring their progress along life's unpredictable path, acknowledging the fluctuations and challenges that may arise. By maintaining this vigilance, people can make informed decisions, adapt to changing circumstances, and proactively steer their lives toward fulfillment and success.

Understanding oneself equips individuals with foresight. Anticipating our own reactions in various situations can prove very beneficial. With self-awareness a person can calculate potential outcomes before plunging into decisions or scenarios. Consequently, self-reflection emerges as a cornerstone of self-control, sound judgment, and gaining insight into one's identity and prospects. It serves as a compass for making informed choices aligned with personal values, thereby nurturing character development and enhancing life navigation skills. However, awareness as we self-analyze is key.

It's essential to approach self-reflection with compassion rather than harsh criticism. The goal is to identify areas for improvement, but this shouldn't lead to self-berating or negative labeling over perceived shortcomings. Deviating from your preferred behavior doesn't warrant self-loathing. Instead, the true purpose of self-reflection is to learn from mistakes and grow from them.

Self-reflection should not turn into unhealthy comparisons or self-deprecation. If such patterns arise, it's crucial to reassess your approach. Being honest and open with yourself is key, as self-deception only hinders genuine growth. By maintaining an empathetic and realistic perspective, self-reflection becomes a powerful tool for personal development rather than a source of unnecessary self-defeatism.

Conversation with Yourself

The essence of self-reflection lies in confronting oneself as if encountering a different person and bravely posing questions that might typically be avoided. It involves summoning the courage to address uncomfortable truths and exploring neglected corners of the psyche, even if they provoke unwelcome emotions. Challenge yourself with questions like, "Why was I so hard on myself today?" and listen attentively to the response, identifying areas for behavioral improvement. Other useful kinds of question to ask are, "What made me feel frustrated when ________________ happened today?" Or, "Why did I respond to ______________ the way I did?"

To facilitate this process, envision yourself evaluating an entirely distinct individual who possesses the same attributes as you, under scrutiny. Perhaps assign this hypothetical persona a pseudonym that resonates with your idealized self. By adopting this perspective, you can detach from personal biases and evaluate your actions with greater objectivity and empathy.

Meditation is widely acclaimed as an effective method for self-reflection. By immersing oneself in a tranquil setting and allowing the mind to explore its thoughts, profound revelations about one's current lifestyle, and emotional well-being, new understandings can emerge. The serenity and stillness inherent in meditation also have the remarkable ability to bring forth emotions that may have been buried deep within the subconscious.

Fully embracing these new feelings and allowing oneself to experience and respond to them, rather than suppressing them, is not only healthy but necessary for personal and professional growth. Confronting emotions can be uncomfortable. Many people prefer to avoid facing certain feelings directly, but pushing past the discomfort can prove healing.

One of the most effective and well-established methods for managing emotions is through writing. Keeping a journal and expressing thoughts and feelings provides a safe outlet for processing emotions without fear of judgment. It offers a sense of solace, akin to confiding in a supportive friend who provides warmth and reassurance.

Through self-reflection, you can identify areas where virtuous character traits may be lacking. For instance, as you wind down at the end of the day, questioning yourself about potential missteps, self-reflection might reveal instances where honesty was compromised. This introspection could trigger a series of realizations, prompting you to acknowledge repeated acts of dishonesty and recognize the need to prioritize honesty as a fundamental character trait.

Following *The Character Blueprint* not only leads to success and meaningful connections but also commands respect from those around you. Character serves as a guiding light that leads to favorable outcomes in both personal and professional circumstances.

When you confront your strengths *and* weaknesses, you gain confidence, but also clarity on areas that need improvement and refinement. You see opportunities and threats. This process not only promotes personal growth but also contributes significantly to enhancing the organizational environment where you work.

Recognizing that individual character impacts not only personal spheres but also dynamics within a professional setting prompts a reassessment of one's weaknesses. Your flaws can have a ripple effect throughout your organization, influencing not only productivity but also the well-being of coworkers.

While a combination of diverse strengths typically leads to optimal outcomes for organizational success, individual weaknesses can pose significant obstacles. For instance, deficient time management skills in a team leader or manager can disrupt workflows and diminish efficiency.

Every team member's character traits play a pivotal role in the collective successes and failures of an organization. Therefore, it becomes imperative to cultivate and leverage the best of each person. Acknowledging that no one excels in everything stresses the importance of self-reflection. Through introspection, individuals can identify areas for growth or where someone else can fill their gaps, supporting overall improvement in teamwork and organizational effectiveness.

The success of any esteemed organization hinges upon the remarkable abilities of individuals and how those abilities synergize within a team to drive favorable outcomes. Therefore, it is imperative that the core values and character traits of each individual align with those of their team, all of which should be in harmony with the overarching goals of the organization.

Various methods exist for evaluating an individual's character, with personality self-assessment tools standing out as particularly effective. These resources facilitate a deeper understanding of one's inherent traits, helping individuals discover their unique essence.

These tools are widely used in professional settings and are remarkably straightforward to employ. They do not require elaborate setups. Instead, they are commonly administered within professional contexts, often by HR personnel or during training sessions, such as talent recruitment and performance assessments.

Assessment tools offer significant benefits not only to employers but to employees as well. For employers, these tools aid in identifying candidates who align with the organization's objectives and cultural ethos, ensuring a suitable fit for a role. Meanwhile, employees can leverage these tools to identify organizations that offer opportunities for skill refinement and talent development, facilitating their professional growth and advancement.

Character and personality assessments are employed to categorize individuals into specific personality types. The following are commonly used.

Myers-Briggs Type Indicator (MBTI)

The Myers-Briggs Type Indicator (MBTI) test is a widely used personality assessment tool designed to identify an individual's psychological preferences in how they perceive the world and make decisions. Developed by Isabel Briggs Myers and her mother, Katharine Cook Briggs, based on the theories of Swiss psychiatrist Carl Jung, the MBTI is grounded in the belief that people have innate preferences that influence their behavior and interactions.

The test categorizes individuals into one of 16 personality types based on four dichotomies:

Extraversion (E) vs. Introversion (I): Extraversion refers to being outgoing, sociable, and energized by external stimulation, while Introversion pertains to being reserved, reflective, and energized by internal thoughts and feelings.

Sensing (S) vs. Intuition (N): Sensing involves focusing on concrete details and practical realities, while Intuition involves focusing on abstract concepts and possibilities.

Thinking (T) vs. Feeling (F): Thinking individuals prioritize logic and objective analysis in decision-making, whereas Feeling individuals prioritize empathy, values, and emotional considerations.

Judging (J) vs. Perceiving (P): Judging individuals prefer structure, planning, and decisiveness, while Perceiving individuals prefer flexibility, spontaneity, and openness to new information.

Through a series of questions, participants indicate their preferences within each dichotomy, leading to the determination of their MBTI type. Each type is represented by a four-letter code, such as "INFJ" or "ESTP," reflecting their preferences across the four dichotomies. Imagine standing at a crossroads, where each path leads in a different direction. You pause for a moment, considering which way feels more natural to walk down. This is like the moment of choice: two options, each pulling in its own way, but only one feels like home.

The MBTI is often used in various contexts, including personal development, career counseling, team building, and organizational development. While it offers valuable insights into personality preferences, it is essential to recognize that it provides a broad framework and does not capture the full complexity of individual personalities. Additionally, critics argue that the MBTI lacks scientific validity and reliability, as it relies on self-reported data and may oversimplify the intricacies of human behavior. Nonetheless, many individuals find the MBTI to be a useful tool for self-awareness and understanding interpersonal dynamics.

DISC Assessment

The DISC assessment is a popular personality assessment tool used to evaluate behavioral preferences and communication styles. Developed by psychologist William

Moulton Marston in the 1920s, the DISC model categorizes individuals into four primary behavioral styles: Dominance (D), Influence (I), Steadiness (S), and Conscientiousness (C). These four dimensions capture different aspects of behavior and provide insights into how individuals interact with others and approach tasks.

Here's an overview of each dimension:

Dominance (D): Individuals with a dominant style tend to be assertive, decisive, and results-oriented. They are often direct communicators who focus on achieving goals and taking charge of situations.

Influence (I): Those with an influential style are outgoing, enthusiastic, and sociable. They excel in building relationships, motivating others, and persuading people to act.

Steadiness (S): Individuals with a steady style are cooperative, patient, and reliable. They prioritize harmony, stability, and teamwork, often providing support and maintaining a calm demeanor in challenging situations.

Conscientiousness (C): Those with a conscientious style are analytical, detail-oriented, and systematic. They value accuracy, organization, and precision, often focusing on quality and adhering to established procedures.

The DISC assessment typically involves answering a series of questions or scenarios to determine one's behavioral tendencies across these four dimensions. Based on the responses, individuals receive a profile that indicates their primary and secondary behavioral styles, along with insights into their communication preferences, strengths, and areas for development.

Clifton Strengths

The Clifton Strengths assessment, also known as StrengthsFinder, is a popular tool developed by Gallup, based on research by psychologist Donald O. Clifton. This assessment aims to identify an individual's unique strengths or talents and provides insights into how they can leverage these strengths to achieve personal and professional success.

The Clifton Strengths assessment measures 34 distinct "themes" or talent themes representing patterns of thought, feeling, and behavior. These themes are organized into four domains:

Executing: Themes in this domain involve taking action and achieving results. Examples include Achiever, Discipline, and Responsibility.

Influencing: Themes in this domain relate to influencing others and driving change. Examples include Communication, Woo (Winning Others Over), and Activator.

Relationship Building: Themes in this domain focus on building and nurturing relationships. Examples include Empathy, Developer, and Relator.

Strategic Thinking: Themes in this domain involve thinking strategically and solving complex problems. Examples include Strategic, Analytical, and Futuristic.

Individuals complete the assessment by responding to a series of statements or questions, indicating the extent to which each statement applies to them. Based on their responses, they receive a personalized report outlining their top five or all 34 talent themes in rank order.

The Clifton Strengths assessment emphasizes the importance of developing and applying one's strengths rather than focusing on weaknesses. It encourages individuals to understand and embrace their unique talents and find opportunities to use them in various aspects of their lives, including their careers, relationships, and personal development.

How are All These Tools Effective in a Business Setting?

The Myers-Briggs Type Indicator (MBTI), DISC assessment, and Clifton Strengths assessment each offer unique insights into individual behavior, communication styles, and talents, making them valuable tools in a business setting. Here's how each assessment can be beneficial and effective:

Myers-Briggs Type Indicator (MBTI):

Enhancing Team Dynamics

Helps team members understand each other's preferences in communication, decision-making, and problem-solving, generating better collaboration and teamwork.

Leadership Development

Assists in identifying leadership styles and preferences, enabling organizations to develop effective leadership training programs tailored to individual needs.

Career Development

Provides valuable insights into individuals' career interests, preferences, and work environments, aiding in career planning, job matching, and talent retention.

DISC Assessment

Improving Communication

Helps individuals understand their own communication styles and those of others, facilitating more effective communication, conflict resolution, and negotiation skills.

Team Building

Identifies complementary strengths and preferences within teams, enabling better alignment of tasks and responsibilities and enhancing overall team performance.

Sales and Customer Service

Used to train sales and customer service teams to adapt their communication styles to better connect with clients and customers, leading to improved customer satisfaction and sales outcomes.

Clifton Strengths Assessment

Maximizing Talent

Helps individuals identify their unique talents and strengths, empowering them to leverage these strengths in their roles, leading to increased engagement, productivity, and job satisfaction.

Team Development

Identifies diverse talents within teams, enabling leaders to build well-rounded teams and assign tasks according to individuals' strengths, ultimately enhancing team performance and innovation.

Leadership Coaching

Used in leadership coaching and development programs to help leaders understand and leverage their strengths to become more effective and authentic leaders.

Each assessment offers valuable insights that can be leveraged to enhance team dynamics, improve communication, maximize talent, and drive organizational success in various aspects of business operations. When used thoughtfully and in conjunction with other organizational development strategies, these assessments can contribute significantly to a positive and productive work environment.

An objective of any team is to recruit individuals whose character traits align with the company's goals, ensuring optimal results. Assessment tools serve as foundational questionnaires utilized by businesses to evaluate individuals' characters and determine their suitability for specific roles.

Hiring Management

These assessments serve as integral components of the hiring process, facilitating the identification of capable individuals. By assessing the character type of candidates, businesses can efficiently categorize whether they are a suitable fit for the company.

Organizational Success

Recruiting individuals who possess qualities conducive to contributing to the business's success is paramount for fostering organizational prosperity. Each hire plays a vital role in shaping the trajectory of the company and its potential for achievement.

Improving Company Culture

Cultivating a cohesive company culture is essential for maintaining organizational identity and values. Bringing together individuals with aligned cultural perspectives spurs collaboration and unity, safeguarding the company's core values and overarching objectives.

Through self-reflection, individuals wield the power to steer their organizations toward success. Recognizing and addressing personal weaknesses while leveraging strengths are key steps toward both individual and organizational growth. As individuals strive for self-improvement, they concurrently bolster the collective strength of the organization, paving the way for sustained success on a broader scale.

Insights from An Old Salt

One of my teams had a bit of a battleground situation going on. We were tasked with auditing programs run by other colleagues. Sounds simple, right? However, when it came time to share our findings, things got messy. People took the criticism personally, feelings got hurt, and arguments flared up, hindering our ability to get anything resolved.

Around this time, during my training to become a Leadership Development Facilitator, I was learning about a tool called the DISC assessment. It seemed like it could be just what we needed. So, I suggested the team take the assessment together.

The results weren't exactly a surprise. It turns out we all had different ways of communicating. Some of us liked things clear and direct with facts, while others needed a different approach that focused more about how the necessary changes affected our people. No wonder our audits were turning into emotional minefields!

The DISC assessment wasn't a magic solution, but it did create a turning point for our team. We finally started talking openly about how we communicated best. We learned to adjust how we delivered information depending on who we were talking to. Slowly but surely, those tense audit meetings turned into helpful brainstorming sessions where we worked together to fix problems. It wasn't always easy, and old habits die hard, but things improved. By understanding each other better, we were finally able to communicate effectively and build stronger relationships as a team.

We all know there is an art to giving criticism in such a way, so it is "well received." By first self-assessing to check our own perspectives and motives and then envisioning ourselves presenting in a way that others can relate to, we can make *The Character Blueprint* work for the greatest good.

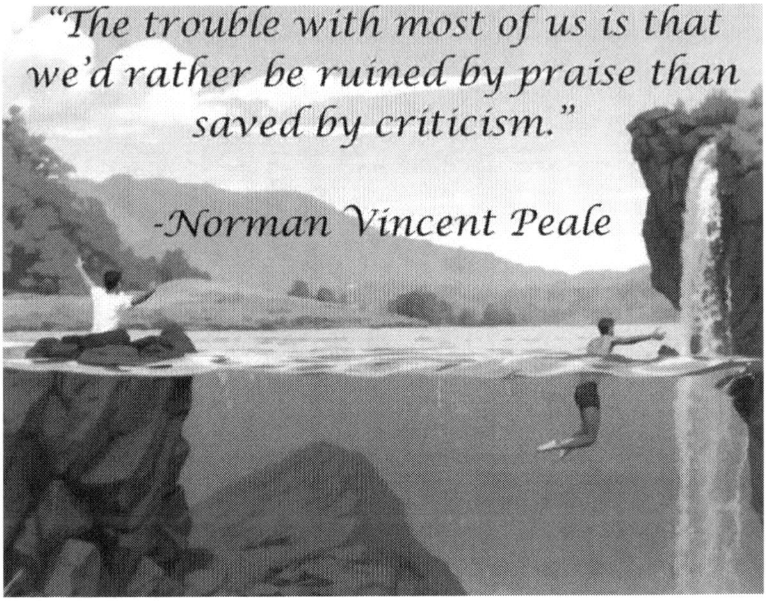

Chapter 4: Integrity as the Cornerstone of Character

Integrity is the quality of being honest and having strong moral principles that you refuse to change. It means to express and live by your values in a way that they are heard and remain consistent. Thus, to present opinions that matter, you need to feel confident in your beliefs and core values.

Being honest with yourself and not straying from those values is the best definition of having integrity as a character trait.

"Leading with integrity and empathy requires vision and a connection to your deepest self."

-Karla McLaren

Integrity acts as a cornerstone for ethical behavior. It shapes the very way we approach the world. While many may possess a collection of admirable traits, a person lacking integrity ultimately undermines trust, damages relationships, and compromises their credibility, leading to long-term negative consequences both personally and professionally.

Integrity follows principles that explain the person's way of living.

A person's moral principles are developed throughout their life, by polishing personal values and core beliefs, evidenced in their actions.

Integrity isn't about blind certainty or perfection. It's the unwavering core that allows you to take ownership of your choices, even when faced with doubt. A person of integrity makes decisions aligned with their values, and that conviction brings a deep sense of pride. Life throws tough choices our way, but integrity assures that you follow your moral compass, even when you are faced with difficult decisions. It's the quiet satisfaction of knowing you stayed true to yourself. Thus, you can take comfort in the fact you followed your beliefs and did not stray away from the values you have dedicated yourself to, allowing you to move through life ethically. Remaining true to our inner values provides immense peace.

Integrity in Business

Integrity serves as the bedrock of trust within a business environment, profoundly influencing customer confidence, employee morale, and the long-term sustainability of the organization. Within the intricate web of business interactions, integrity becomes paramount, regardless of one's position within the company. From the CEO to front line employees, each action an individual takes reverberates throughout the organization, shaping its credibility and reputation.

Smart business leaders place immense value on individuals who display unwavering integrity and strong character traits. Such individuals exhibit accountability and responsibility for their tasks, willingly accepting both credit and repercussions, as circumstances warrant. For instance, when faced with a situation where an important member is grappling with health issues, a manager's response emphasizes the organization's values. By demonstrating empathy and offering flexibility with working hours or time off, the manager not only showcases integrity but also signals the organization's commitment to valuing its employees.

Furthermore, confidentiality becomes paramount in creating a culture of trust and respect. When an employee confides in a coworker, upholding confidentiality becomes an expression of integrity. Respect for privacy not only cultivates trust among coworkers but also stimulates a peaceful and harmonious work environment.

Conversely, hypocrisy, the antithesis of integrity, poses a significant threat to organizational success. In a landscape fraught with risks, integrity becomes indispensable for fueling honesty and confidence. Having unwavering faith and support in the people we work with enables us to navigate risky decisions, knowing there's a safety net to fall back on. In essence, integrity becomes a linchpin for organizational success, anchoring it amidst the tumultuous seas of business challenges.

Moreover, individuals who embody strong personal character and adhere to an ethical code of conduct brighten the workplace with a distinct perspective. As an integral component of teamwork, integrity prompts successful collaborative efforts, driving both individual and collective achievements for long-term sustained success.

Understanding the importance of integrity in teamwork and the crucial aspect of its implementation goes hand in hand with achieving successful results. Integrity requires having honesty as the core principle. Upholding honesty in both work habits and communication ensures a conducive and transparent working environment, which is crucial for effective collaboration.

As individuals with integrity, it is imperative to understand and respect the diverse opinions and perspectives of other team members. By refraining from imposing our personal beliefs and instead encouraging an environment that values different talents and viewpoints, mutual respect is achieved.

When both the individual and the team embody integrity as a foundation for their values and beliefs, shared perspectives serve as a driving force. This benefits the business positively and reinforces its mission and objectives.

When considering team integrity, accountability is paramount. Recognizing and appreciating the efforts of team members while taking responsibility for one's own actions builds trust and cohesion. This sense of accountability ensures that individuals uphold ethical standards and contribute to the collective success of the business and the people who work there.

Without trust, team members may hesitate to rely on one another, leading to inefficiencies and communication breakdowns. Accountability ensures that everyone takes ownership of their roles and contributions, which promotes reliability and a sense of responsibility across the group.

Integrity in teamwork mirrors the foundational principles of business ethics. By prioritizing integrity as a central character trait, teams cultivate a positive work environment conducive to maximum efficiency and productivity.

Integrity in Business Ethics

In addition to trust and accountability, there are other ethical attributes required for a team to not only succeed, but to endure the daily challenges thrown their way. These ethics are respect and transparency.

Respect is essential to maintain a positive, inclusive atmosphere where diverse perspectives are valued. This prevents conflicts and encourages creative problem-solving. Transparency is equally important, as it builds a foundation of openness and honesty, allowing team members to address challenges directly rather than avoiding or hiding them.

When these ethical principles are upheld, a team can remain cohesive, motivated, and resilient, even in the face of adversity. Without them, trust erodes, misunderstandings grow, and the team risks falling apart under pressure.

Building Trust Through Ethical Work

With integrity as an inherent character trait, we cultivate trust and credibility within the work environment. Coworkers and peers see each other as reliable individuals entrusted with sensitive company information.

Acknowledging the contributions of others and providing due credit elevates one's reputation as a person of integrity. This practice reinforces trustworthiness and reliability, as colleagues recognize the fair and appreciative nature of their leader.

Ethical conduct necessitates the protection of both customer and coworker privacy, as a matter of integrity. Adhering to an ethical code of conduct involves ensuring the security of others' information, thus strengthening the foundation of trust within the workplace.

Leaders that demonstrate trust and respect toward their employees offer true whistleblower protection. Providing such protection signifies the organization's belief in its employees' commitment to the company's best interests, undergirding a culture of accountability and integrity.

Individuals with strong character traits, including integrity, are highly regarded for their loyalty. A loyal employee consistently adheres to the company's rules and regulations, regardless of tenure. Their dedication and steadfastness contribute significantly to the organization's success and reputation.

Trust in employees enables them to act decisively during challenging circumstances. Micromanagement is eschewed in favor of trusting employees' abilities to navigate crises effectively. This autonomy produces a sense of responsibility and empowerment, further solidifying trust within the organization.

How to Improve Integrity in Teams and Organizations

Teams can implement several key strategies to forge a healthier work environment through heightened integrity

Establishing effective communication is crucial for understanding the thought processes of team members. Promoting transparency and collaboration are essential in creating an environment where employees feel comfortable discussing any topic with both their peers and leadership. When individuals feel they can openly share their ideas, concerns, and feedback without fear of judgment or retribution, a culture of trust and psychological safety emerges. This, in turn, sparks innovation and problem-solving, as employees are more likely to voice opposing perspectives and propose creative solutions.

Moreover, transparency in decision-making processes and expectations helps to eliminate ambiguity, ensuring that everyone is aligned on common goals and objectives. When team members are kept informed about why certain decisions are made, they are more likely to feel valued and connected to the bigger picture. Collaboration thrives when communication is open and frequent, as it allows for the pooling of talents and expertise to tackle complex challenges.

In such an environment, employees not only feel heard but also empowered to take initiative, knowing their contributions are recognized and respected. This level of engagement and mutual respect contributes to higher morale, stronger team dynamics, and ultimately, a more productive and cohesive organization.

Promote an Ethical Code of Conduct

Upholding an ethical code of conduct in the workplace is directly linked to cultivating a culture of integrity and fairness, as both reinforce and sustain each other. This approach provides the formal framework that defines expected behaviors, laying the groundwork for how employees should conduct themselves professionally. When this code is consistently enforced, it creates a foundation of accountability, where integrity and fairness are not just encouraged but required. Employees become aware that unethical behavior, such as dishonesty, discrimination, or favoritism, will not be tolerated. Trust and respect between individuals and departments thrive in an ethical environment, allowing integrity to spread throughout the organization.

If the ethical code is upheld without bias, employees are more likely to believe in the organization's commitment to justice. Integrity thrives in an environment where ethical decisions are made openly and equitably, with employees confident that their efforts and contributions will be evaluated based on merit, not personal connections or unfair advantages. This sense of fairness helps to build stronger interpersonal relationships, teamwork, and loyalty to the organization, as individuals are motivated by a shared sense of moral responsibility.

Moreover, when integrity and fairness are embedded into the daily operations of the workplace, they become part of the organization's identity and reputation. Over time, this ethical culture not only improves internal dynamics but also enhances the organization's credibility with external stakeholders, such as customers, clients, and business partners. In the long run, upholding an ethical code and promoting a culture of integrity and fairness leads to a more resilient, cohesive, and productive workplace, where employees feel respected, valued, and driven to contribute positively.

Taking Swift Action Against Unethical Behavior

Promptly addressing unethical behavior is crucial for promoting ethical practices. Holding individuals accountable and enforcing consequences for misconduct sends a clear message that integrity and ethical behavior are non-negotiable values within the organization. This approach reinforces the seriousness of ethical standards and strengthens the overall commitment to a culture of responsibility.

Acknowledge and Reward Integrity

Recognizing individuals who demonstrate integrity and contribute to improving the productivity of the work environment is essential. By acknowledging their efforts and appreciating their commitment to ethical conduct, organizations reinforce the value of integrity.

Lead By Example

Managers play a crucial role in promoting integrity within their teams. By consistently demonstrating a strong belief in ethical principles and leading by example, managers inspire their team members to uphold similar values. This fosters a culture where integrity is prioritized and respected by all.

In both personal and professional life, integrity serves as a fundamental tool for building a reputable character. Respect, earned through consistent displays of integrity, is a testament to one's strong character. Integrity acts as a bridge between respect and trust, empowering individuals to rely on each other's actions and decisions. Building integrity requires time and consistency, demonstrated through commitment and honesty in all situations. Ultimately, a person of integrity not only earns respect but also gains the invaluable gift of trust from those around them.

Insights from An Old Salt

A supervisor accidentally turned off a crucial piece of equipment during a critical process. Initially, instead of owning up to the mistake, this supervisor attempted to shift blame onto a subordinate and told them they wouldn't get into trouble because "they don't know any better."

However, to my surprise, the subordinate came forward and reported the supervisor's instructions to take the blame despite not being responsible for the incident. The subordinate expressed discomfort with the idea of taking undeserved blame and wanted to stand up for what was right.

This incident highlights a clear breach of integrity on the supervisor's part. Leadership swiftly acted, recognizing the importance of accountability. As a result, the supervisor was released from their position due to a loss of confidence in their ability to uphold the organization's values and standards.

This scenario serves as a powerful reminder of the importance of integrity in leadership roles, and the consequences that can arise when individuals fail to adhere to ethical principles. It also accentuates the significance of employees who demonstrate courage and integrity by speaking up against wrongdoing, even in challenging situations.

Chapter 5: Developing Emotional Intelligence for Effective Collaboration

Emotional Intelligence (EI) or Emotional Quotient (EQ) is the ability to understand, process, and handle emotions in a healthy manner. This not only includes a person's own emotions but also the feelings of others as well.

While 50-80% of a person's cognitive abilities, including the IQ level, are heredity, emotional intelligence is built through different factors. It is a basic life component seen in individuals who are successful in life. Some people thrive, while some might fail when faced with difficult tasks, depending on a person's emotional intelligence.

There is no certain age that determines when a person becomes emotionally intelligent. Nor can you predict how long it takes to develop emotional maturity; it is something formed through experiences and by learning to control the steering of your own life.

According to Stephen Covey, author of *The Seven Habits of Highly Effective People*, different aspects are counted in the reasons accounting for emotional intelligence:

"Every human has four endowments - self-awareness, conscience, independent will, and creative imagination. These give us the ultimate human freedom... The power to choose, to respond, to change."

-Stephen Covey

Self-awareness is the first basic step toward trying to evaluate your emotional intelligence. Studying how you react to certain feelings in different circumstances is essential. When you are sad, do you go completely quiet or tend to break out in tears in the agony of the moment? Each person has their own defined way of reacting to emotional triggers.

It is important to understand how you process emotions if you are to make sense of the outcomes resulting from your actions. If unwanted behavioral outbursts are a problem, you will want to make changes in how you process your feelings.

For example, a person with anger issues could take time out of their day to try and understand what triggered that reaction in them.

After learning about your emotions, it is crucial to take measures leading to ways that improve your reaction to those feelings. You can evaluate processing options to determine what works best for you. It could be meditation, seeking therapy, journaling, outdoor walks, deep breathing, and so on.

Being emotionally intelligent also means being empathic toward others and patient with yourself. In some instances, you may find you disregard your own emotions, judging yourself to be overdramatic, for example. Treating yourself harshly or rigidly should be avoided.

Moreover, discovering emotional intelligence means listening to what other people have to say and exhibiting authentic compassion. It is important to take into consideration the opinions of others. You could ask someone how your behavior has impacted them. You can check yourself to ensure you don't overreact when another person expresses that you have hurt them or when they ask for help. You should know how to listen to people's problems without jumping to conclusions or immediately presenting solutions.

Emotional intelligence is mainly judged on the persona you show in public. Most of the conclusions about personality are made after someone's first interaction with us. Thus, the way you move through a social setting displays your emotional spectrum and intelligence.

If a person has no friends and always turns down the offer to hang out with nice people, that could make his character questionable or even unlikeable. Having the skill of building relationships and communicating effectively highlights emotional intelligence.

Importance of Emotional Intelligence

Emotional intelligence is important in different aspects of life and work:

Emotional intelligence allows a person to communicate effectively and successfully. It helps you assess verbal and even nonverbal cues.

Communication is the basic building block of any relationship. Thus, having good emotional intelligence would indirectly lead to better communication skills, which is important, personally or professionally.

Emotional intelligence drives healthy relationships. All a person needs from a friend, family member, colleague, or partner is someone who listens and knows how to communicate their feelings in a balanced, objective way. Being emotionally intelligent allows for a person to consider the wrong and right in a relationship by seeking facts and evidence versus simply fighting to be right or to get their own way. An emotionally intelligent person is a mature, solid block who seeks to give, yet is willing to receive. A relationship thrives when two such individuals ebb and flow. Instead of one person emotionally leaning on their partner or colleague for the most part, which can be draining for both, each contributes consistently to meet the needs of the other.

Another important aspect of emotional intelligence is the ability to manage stress. Under stressful conditions, someone can make rash decisions or treat others poorly. Whether leading at home, in your community, or at the workplace, effectively managing stress and not lashing out or reacting impulsively produce healthy relationships and environments.

Indecisiveness and making the wrong decisions out of fear can also lead to unanticipated and unwanted consequences. Exercising intentionality to become aware of your emotions and knowing what to do to improve your behavior, can help you make decisions that are beneficial for yourself and others.

Emotional Intelligence in Teamwork

You might wonder how emotional intelligence blends with organizational or team success.

As I've previously stated, the success of a team is based on each person's contribution. Group abilities are determined by the emotional intelligence of each person involved.

The emotional intelligence of collective members determines the productivity and efficacy of the teamwork. Certain aspects of tasks or projects often depend on each person's emotional constitution and determine the result of a team's efforts.

Consider a manager who struggles to communicate a task properly to an employee or an employee who does not know how to communicate and ask for help. This creates a communication gap that affects the performance of the team. Emotional intelligence leads to healthy and enhanced communication that improves the relationship between team members.

Good communication leads to collaboration that helps improve the quality of work. Certain tasks work better with the cooperative efforts of individuals on the team.

Having a person who is emotionally intelligent and strong allows them to adjust to conditions that might not be favorable or that may be out of their comfort zone. Only a person showcasing objective skills and emotional intelligence can take up challenging conditions and tasks.

A person who can deal with unexpected situations in a healthy way is a crucial treasure for a team. Each individual should have enough emotional intelligence to work at solving any problems, including those that blindside them. A person who is firm in the face of adverse situations and resolute in seeking solutions instead of adding to problems is vital for the success of the team.

An individual with emotional maturity feels the freedom to wander off and explore ideas that others might not even consider. This innovative part of their thoughts, and their ability to take risks, leads to imaginative outcomes and creative solutions.

Though true that a healthy work environment requires good communication, collaborative efforts, and constructive criticism, it also includes being able to take a joke and lighten up the work environment, when appropriate. An uptight attitude and only focusing on filling in the work hours like a robot stimulates a machinelike atmosphere that usually leads to lower morale, resentment, and burnout.

Leaders who follow *The Character Blueprint* know how to deal with the team members they are responsible for, based on each individual's emotional spectrum. This approach promotes a healthy work environment with high odds of great success, because people are treated like the human beings that they are.

Why is a Good Team Relationship Necessary?

Any organizational success is completely dependent on how well a team progresses together. Putting a team together in a way that works best provides maximum quality. But an astute leader knows their team will need ongoing motivation for productivity, which is both tricky and vital.

The people who make up a team should be able to communicate openly with emotional presence around their coworkers. In order to be a vital coworker, a good person must first possess strong character based on morals and principles that are in the best interest of the success of the organization.

Different people of varying personalities and perspectives cannot work together unless they have a mindset for achieving the same goal. Consider a game of football where the score is tied by a touchdown in its last minutes. There are two options for the coach to play. In one, the emphasis is on protecting the kicker with a defensive lineup to complete the mission of safely bagging the one extra point by field goal. Or secondly, the coach encourages the team to attack offensively, with a chance of winning by two, after gaining the extra point.

Both coaching strategies are viable options. But if you were to put the two coaches on the same team with strong opposing opinions, it could lead to a conflict. Unless each of them has good enough communication and conflict resolution skills to reach consensus for a practical solution, they are destined to butt heads. Team building is based on mutual maturity, performance, and the ability to identify common grounds, particularly between leaders. People need to respect and connect, so they can bring quality to their work. The approach taken at the top will always move its way down—whether the example is good or bad.

Effective collaboration is built on the bedrock of emotionally intelligent communication, requiring not only attention to verbal aspects but also knowledge of nonverbal cues and aspects. The whole communication channel is made up of listening, understanding, and communicating back clearly.

Being empathetic, holding yourself accountable for your mistakes, giving credit where due, and being polite can help create positive dynamics within a team. These include, but are not limited to:

- A healthy work environment
- Improved quality of work
- Enhanced productivity
- Customer satisfaction
- The company's profits

A team consisting of emotionally intelligent individuals who know how to tackle difficult situations and communicate well with other team members support all of the benefits listed above.

Emotional intelligence is the basic building block for a commendable character, allowing a person to display confidence, humility, and healthy self-esteem. Without these qualities in leadership, organizational success is next to impossible.

Insights from An Old Salt

It was a challenging period within our team. Tensions ran high and conflicts threatened to derail our progress. The consequences of the task before us were truly a matter of national security. We could not risk the in-fighting that threatened to undermine the mission.

During this time, our manager, known for his exceptional emotional intelligence, stepped in to defuse the situation. With a calm demeanor and empathetic approach, he took the time to actively listen, allowing each party's concerns and perspectives to be heard without fear of judgment. By acknowledging the validity of each viewpoint and encouraging open dialogue, our manager created a safe space for constructive communication. Through patient mediation and guidance, they facilitated a resolution that not only addressed the immediate conflict but also strengthened our team dynamics. This helped us deal with the present situation in the best way possible, while also equipping us for faster and higher level success in future missions we would undertake.

This experience left a lasting impression on me. Our manager's willingness to listen, without interjecting their own ego or any personal insecurities, underscored the profound impact of emotional intelligence in restoring cohesiveness to a team. By their example, they gave the rest of us permission to respond with like-minded confidence and listening ears.

"Leadership is all about emotional intelligence. Management is taught, while leadership is experienced."

-Rajeev Suri

IQ + EQ = SUCCESS

Chapter 6: Cultivating Resilience and Adaptability

Resilience isn't just about bouncing back from life's setbacks; it's about embodying strength and fortitude when faced with adversity. While some may perceive resilience as turning a blind eye to problems, it's quite the contrary. True resilience involves confronting challenges head-on, maintaining composure, and actively seeking solutions rather than succumbing to defeat.

Think of resilience as a skill honed over time rather than an innate trait. It's something we cultivate through life's experiences, not something we're inherently born with. And there's a myriad of ways to weave resilience into our daily lives, making it a powerful tool for navigating life's complexities.

In the midst of hardship, it's tempting to simplify matters with a dismissive "just get over it." But resilience demands more than mere platitudes. Resilience requires a profound mental strength to persevere in the face of setbacks. It's the secret sauce that empowers us to overcome life's toughest trials and emerge stronger on the other side.

"When nobody fails, everybody loses.

Feedback and resilience are vital."

-Alan Froggatt

There are multiple facets to nurturing resilience within ourselves. *The Character Blueprint* understands the importance of developing fortitude in each of the following ways, becoming:

- Mentally resilient
- Emotionally resilient
- Physically resilient
- Socially resilient

Picture mental and emotional resilience as a dynamic duo, wielding the power to navigate life's storms with serene strength. It's about more than just weathering hardships—it's about calmly assessing adversity and effortlessly maintaining composure. An emotionally resilient individual doesn't just ride the waves of their feelings; they skillfully steer their emotions toward positivity and productive energy.

On the physical front, resilience manifests as the body's ability to rebound from the rigors it faces—whether illness, exhaustion, or burnout. Intentionality in motivating yourself to physical activity when all you want to do is veg out on the couch and play video games or watch a movie demonstrates resilience.

And in the social sphere, resilience finds its footing in the supportive embrace of community, whether through social groups or other forms of camaraderie. Choosing to engage with others versus hiding out or hermitizing on the heels of a challenging circumstance makes you socially resilient.

Like so many qualities of *The Character Blueprint*, resilience isn't a trait we're born with, it's a masterpiece crafted through the canvas of life's challenges. Resilience is about embracing change and mastering the art of healthy emotional management despite the unexpected or difficult.

But *The Character Blueprint* isn't solely about weathering the storm—it's also about dancing in the rain. It's the symbiotic relationship between adaptability and resilience, where one's ability to thrive in adversity is rooted in their capacity to flex and adjust. It's about turning unforeseen challenges into opportunities for growth and triumph.

Imagine you're deep under the ocean, hundreds of meters below the surface, surrounded by steel walls as thick as your forearm, in the dimly lit confines of a submarine. You've been submerged for nearly two months, running drills and routines on a vessel packed with machinery and crew, with little space for unconstructed movement. Then, halfway through a three-month patrol, an unexpected mechanical failure occurs—the oxygen generator malfunctions. Air quality quickly begins to decline. Every breath feels a little heavier than the one before—a little closer, tinged with the subtle tang of recycled air. The odds are high that to a man, each has to push fleeting thoughts away, making them wonder if they will soon breathe their last.

Prior to this event, everyone's nerves were already on edge. Weeks in tight quarters have sharpened even the smallest irritations, and now you face a test that's equal parts mental and physical. But you are in the military, trained to anticipate issues and adapt quickly under pressure.

Together, the crew kicks into action. The mechanics work tirelessly on temporary repairs, adapting makeshift filters from whatever components they can find available onboard. The cooks modify the menu to lessen oxygen use in cooking. Others initiate emergency drills to keep sharp and ready for anything, while everyone focuses on lessening their inhalations and exhalations to stay alive.

Communication is brief, calm, and direct. There's no room for error or emotional fray. In these confined quarters, it's as much about self-discipline as it is about teamwork.

In such situations, each submariner adapts individually, finding unique ways to keep morale up, such as short jokes to break the tension. Camaraderie in shared tasks is a must. As you learn to control your breathing, to slow down every action to conserve energy—you find resilience in adjusting your body, mind, and spirit to the situation.

Days pass under these conditions. Then, finally, the generator is fixed. Fresh air flows in, filling every compartment. Each sailor feels the relief. Reflecting on what you experienced, you see that resilience and adaptability were key. Despite the challenges, the team pulled through, adjusting quickly and supporting one another.

In the uncertainties of life, adaptability brings us both success and survival. In a world where the unexpected lurks around every corner, it's the resilient, adaptable souls who emerge victorious, turning adversity into stepping stones toward greatness.

Navigating through challenges often demands not just expertise but also a character compass. Ethical dilemmas frequently loom in business, calling for individuals with sharp analytical minds, problem-solving prowess, and an unwavering sense of composure to step up and lead with moral certainty.

Amidst a sea of credentials and accolades, it's the often-overlooked traits of resilience and adaptability that emerge as the unsung heroes of professional success. Firm yet flexible leadership draw clear lines in *The Character Blueprint*.

Maya and Her Diamonds

At Nexus Innovations, a tech firm known for its fast-paced projects and ambitious timelines, chaos was the norm. Every Monday morning, employees braced themselves for a whirlwind of tasks, deadlines, and unexpected changes. Among them was Maya, a project manager who often wondered how anyone could thrive in such an environment. Yet, this was where she learned that order could be found in chaos, stress could be mastered, and mistakes could forge diamonds.

The first sign of disorder usually arrived with the morning briefing. Reports often relayed shifting stakeholders' demands, or the group was told a timeline had shortened yet again. Maya's team would sit around the table, feeling the weight of another impossible week. Initially, Maya panicked in these moments, but no longer. She had learned that in chaos, there's always a pattern waiting to be discovered—or created.

Maya began gathering her team and breaking the messy reports down into digestible details. Tasks were divided and reorganized, priorities were reassessed, until the mountain of confusion became a series of steps the group could climb together.

Maya's method wasn't magic, but it was a process. She found small points of order within the overarching chaos and emphasized them to those she led making the situation feel more manageable. Each team member was encouraged to voice concerns or potential hurdles, and as they worked together, clarity emerged. Nexus didn't slow down for them, but Maya's team learned to carve out moments of calm within the stormy Monday sessions.

Still, stress was inevitable. As deadlines loomed, work piled up, and expectations rose. Team burnout looked inevitable. That was where Maya's second lesson came in.

Nexus was relentless, but Maya knew that if her team was to survive, they needed space to breathe. She implemented micro-breaks, short, five-minute pauses every hour where people could step away from their screens, stretch, or chat with a colleague. It seemed small, but it made a huge difference. Maya was teaching her people to master the stresses through work-life balance in incremental strides.

Maya also encouraged flexible working hours. As long as the team met their deliverables, they could adjust their schedules to suit their personal lives. This was vital for team member Javier, a father of two young children, who often needed to move his workday hours for family commitments. The flexibility allowed the team to manage their stresses without compromising on their responsibilities, turning what could have been overwhelming pressure into something they could navigate. It also proved a great morale booster, as employees felt cared for and heard.

But perhaps the most transformative lesson Maya learned came from mistakes. In the fast-moving world of tech, errors were inevitable. Once, a new feature went live with a major bug. Another time, an important client presentation was delayed with little notice because of miscommunication. Each mistake felt like a disaster in the moment, but it was in those times of failure that the team learned their most valuable lessons.

Maya coined the term "forging diamonds" for the process. She explained that every mistake became an opportunity to refine, to look at what had gone wrong, and to find the spark of improvement within it. After the bug debacle, they restructured their testing protocols, ensuring every future release went through a rigorous review beforehand. When the presentation delay happened, they developed clearer communication channels, leaving no room for new misunderstandings.

Maya fostered an environment where mistakes weren't feared but embraced. The team began to share their slip-ups openly, knowing that each one would lead to growth. Rather than letting errors tear them down, they allowed their flaws to convert them into a stronger, more resilient team. In time, they became known for their innovation and versatility, their ability to turn setbacks into opportunities. They thrived where others faltered.

By the end of the year, Maya's team had transformed. What had once seemed like chaos now looked like a series of challenges to be mastered. Her people had learned to balance the stresses of their work with the needs of their lives, and they had emerged stronger from their mistakes. Like diamonds forged under pressure, they had become polished, resilient, and brilliant.

In the heart of Nexus Innovations, where the storm never ceased, Maya's team stood firm. They found solutions in their problems and shone in the crucible of stress and failure. In their hands, every mistake became a diamond.

Shiv Nadar, the visionary behind HCL Technologies, once said, "Adaptability and constant innovation are key to the survival of any company operating in a competitive market." His words echo the sentiment that openness to change isn't just a trait we should desire; it's the heart of a thriving team and growing organization.

Imagine a team where each member seamlessly adjusts to the demands of the moment, where adaptability isn't just a skill—it's a way of life. In such an environment, the quality of work soars, individual talents shine, and efficiency becomes second nature. Trust flourishes, relationships deepen, and together, people weather disturbances that would crush less limber teams.

Adaptability improves many qualities, such as:

- Excellence in work

- Individual skills
- Work efficiency
- Employee performance
- Good relations between team members
- Trust and reliance
- Risk management
- Emotional support

But how does one cultivate such a culture of adaptability? It starts with leadership. Captains who steer their crew toward challenges through guidance and encouragement, show people how to stretch without snapping. They help team members to see their own abilities through the leader's belief in them. Clarity of purpose is essential—and when a leader acknowledges the magnitude of the task at hand, everyone understands the stakes.

Yet, adaptability isn't just about reacting. It's about proactive openness to new ideas and approaches. It's about daring to consider the situation in a unique way, to innovate, and to create breakthroughs where others see only obstacles. And yes, it requires embracing mistakes as those stepping stones toward growth.

In a whirlwind of resilience and adaptability, both individuals and teams find their true strength. Those unafraid to embrace change and push boundaries will flourish in the face of uncertainty.

Under the guidance of leadership following the framework of *The Character Blueprint*, each team member is entrusted with roles tailored to their strengths. This provides individuals with the perfect stage to shine. It's not just about delegation; it's about crafting challenges that elevate skills rather than undermining them.

Consider this scenario: A newcomer joins the team. Assigning them tasks typically completed by seasoned veterans would only set this person up for failure. Instead, a smart leader nurtures the new team member's potential by assigning tasks that gradually build expertise, stair stepping opportunities for them to excel in the future.

It is equally important that any mission tasked to a team be properly discussed beforehand. If a situation is critical and hard to take on, reality should be acknowledged instead of pretending that it will be easily doable. *The Character Blueprint* does not place unnecessary pressure on people.

To be truly adaptable is to embrace the unpredictable with an open mind, daring to venture beyond the confines of what feels comfortable. It's about shattering the rigid boundaries we've erected around problems as protection barriers and realizing that solutions can manifest in unexpected forms when we take risks. It's about daring to forge new paths and conceiving novel approaches that defy convention.

In any workplace, there should be ample space for experimentation and the freedom to follow one's instincts. Mistakes embraced as opportunities for growth and learning shift the focus from regret to resilience and improvement.

Those who dare to follow *The Character Blueprint* tackle diverse challenges head-on and are unafraid to push boundaries. These are the leaders, by title or by actions, poised for success. Timid teams will only find themselves caught in their wake.

Insights from An Old Salt

We've all been on teams where a select few individuals became the go-to problem solvers. These superstars are undeniably valuable. They're competent and efficient—they get things done effectively and correctly. Leaders naturally turn to them first when a tough task needs tackling. However, what seems like a shortcut in the immediate can have detrimental long-term effects on the team.

I've made the mistake of relying solely on star performers, only to create a bottleneck in knowledge and skill transfer. When all the work funneled through a select few people, their expertise became a roadblock to our overall competencies. The rest of the team missed out on valuable learning opportunities. In some cases, people rarely got the chance to develop their own skills or gain experience like our "go-to" people. This would have left our unpracticed people unprepared if key members were no longer on the team. For a while, our team's overall knowledge and capabilities became reliant on a select few, hindering our ability to adapt and grow. Thankfully, by studying successful leaders and through the mentorship I was privileged to receive, I recognized the error of my leadership ways before too much damage was done.

Over-reliance on a select few can also lead those individuals to burnout and resentment. Another danger comes when go-to people become overloaded, constantly shouldering the brunt of the workload. This can spur exhaustion and frustration, ultimately draining them dry. Meanwhile, underutilized team members may feel undervalued and disengage. They see all the important work consistently going to others while their own skills and abilities are unnoticed. This can negatively impact overall morale and productivity. A team environment operating in imbalances is unlikely to accomplish its objectives or meet its potential.

The solution lies in leadership's empowerment of a capable team. By distributing tasks more evenly and providing on-the-job training, you can cultivate a team with a wider range of skills and a stronger overall capability. Each team member gets the opportunity to sharpen their abilities and expertise, making the team more powerful. Balanced learning fosters teamwork and a sense of shared responsibility for everyone's success. In *The Character Blueprint*, a culture of collaboration emerges, where each person feels valued as they contribute to the team's achievements.

Investing in the development of all team members may seem less efficient initially. Training takes time, and new skills require repetition to master. But doing so builds a stronger, more resilient team with an adaptive mindset that can handle unexpected changes and challenges more effectively. In the long run, a well-rounded team with diverse skillsets is far more valuable than a team reliant on a few star performers.

7STEPS
TO A SUCCESSFUL
PEER MENTORSHIP PROGRAM
MENTORSHIP FACILITATOR
• A facilitator will help the process run smoothly.
• They should keep the conversation flowing but not be directly involved.
• It's important they stay neutral, and there is no authority associated with their role.
1
SAFE ENVIRONMENT
• Team members MUST feel comfortable speaking up and sharing their experiences.
• Participants must feel safe to ask questions without fear of being embarrassed.
• Emphasize the importance of respectful communication. The facilitator can help set up a code of conduct.
2
NETWORKING EVENTS
• Networking events aren't all about exchanging business cards, they can be a great source of new perspectives and ideas.
• Set up happy hour meetups, industry seminars, or office mixers.
• Sharing events will help form trust and build valuable connections.
3
DON'T WASTE EXPERIENCE
• Identify seasoned employees to create peer-to-peer learning content for new employees.
• It'll give the newcomers a chance to learn their jobs hands-on and to integrate into the company.
4
COMMONALITY
• Finding the commonality between experiences helps employees relate to one another.
• Employees might be surprised to learn their colleagues have struggled with a similar problem.
• This drives a desire to learn how they overcame the issue.
5
WELCOME DIVERSITY
• Bringing together employees from different backgrounds fosters an open-minded, global company culture.
• This can make them better equipped to see situations from many perspectives.
6
TRACK PROGRESS
• Ask your peer learners for suggestions and feedback on the lessons they have learned.
• Make a note of learners' consumption of the educational content.
• You can use this information for continuously improving peer training programs.
7
THE CHARACTER BLUEPRINT:
Crafting Effective Teams Through Personal Development
www.successthroughself.com

Chapter 7: Building a Culture of Collaboration and Accountability

We've explored the significance of assembling a team packed with strong character traits. Yet, true alchemy occurs when these individuals unite within a supportive environment, reinforced by a robust work ethic, elevating the standard of output for any organization.

However, even after assembling a dream team, there are crucial factors to consider. Ultimately, the greatness of a team is measured by the seamless interplay of its members. Genuine collaboration flourishes when trust binds individuals together, when free-flowing communication is not blocked, and when accountability is expected and embraced.

In *The Character Blueprint*, pivotal elements are understood to affect the relationship between team members. For the organization's health, it is imperative that the following is promoted, repeated, and adhered to:

- Being honest with each other
- Being able to communicate openly
- Trusting all team members
- Not blaming others for your mistakes

Honesty serves as the cornerstone of each interaction, nurturing an environment where true friendships are formed and can thrive. In such a landscape, accountability emerges as a beacon of integrity. A commitment to owning one's actions, learning from missteps, and avoiding the blame game frees us from anxiety, guilt, and regret, and bolsters the confidence others have in us.

Accountability extends beyond the confines of the workplace; it's a fundamental pillar of life itself. To dodge responsibility is to deny growth and stifle your own progress. In the realm of teamwork, evading accountability corrodes confidence and undermines the very foundation upon which successful collaborations are built.

So, let us champion accountability as a guiding principle, forging teams that embody integrity, resilience, and a shared commitment to excellence. In doing so, the people we work alongside know they can count on us, while our self-esteem is strengthened. When we hold ourselves to higher standards, our organizations continue to strive for and reach new zeniths and as individuals, we expand our abilities.

One significant hurdle in teamwork arises when individuals shift blame for their failures onto other team members. Within a collaborative work setting, it's tempting to remain silent and allow the fault to cascade onto your colleagues rather than taking ownership of your actions and acknowledging mistakes. Yet, true growth and productivity can only happen when individuals dare to own up to their errors, extend apologies where needed, and gather valuable lessons from failures. Such accountability safeguards reliability and gives way to more possibilities.

Promoting Collaboration and Accountability in a Team

In the lively realm of group dynamics, collaboration and accountability are not just buzzwords. Even when a team seems to be hitting its stride, there's always room for growth and evolution.

The following is just one example of how our naval men and women are put to the test.

Aboard the USS Defender, the submarine's control room hummed under the quiet focus of the watch team on duty. Lieutenant Sarah Ortiz, the Officer of the Deck, scanned the sonar display. The dim, blue glow reflected on her face as she monitored. Petty Officer Marcus Langley, seated at the sonar console, listened intently for any unusual sounds in the ocean's deep, dark expanse.

They were nearing a classified operation zone, and tensions were high. The captain had stressed the importance of vigilance, as enemy subs had been reported nearby.

"Conn, sonar, contact bearing 235, possible sub," Langley reported, his voice calm but precise.

Ortiz quickly relayed the information. "Helm, come to course 235. Steady as she goes."

As the submarine silently turned, Chief Petty Officer Lena Thompson, supervising the team, noticed a small error on the navigation console.

"Petty Officer Kim," Thompson said firmly, her tone leaving no room for doubt, "Your depth reading is off. Recalibrate now."

Kim's face flushed with embarrassment but nodded, immediately fixing the error.

Thompson gave her a quick nod of approval after checking the updated readings. "Good. Stay focused."

The team worked in seamless coordination, each person trusting the others to do their job but holding each other accountable when needed. There was no time or space for over-sensitivity, our lives depended on working together. Accepting and responding positively to accountability enhanced our odds of a good outcome. The threat of the enemy submarine loomed large, there was no room for ego or error here—only unity and precision.

Suddenly, Langley's voice cut through the quiet. "Conn, sonar, confirmed hostile contact. Closing at 500 yards."

Ortiz reacted instantly. "Rig for silent running. All stations, maintain quiet and hold positions."

The team moved quickly, each action synchronized like clockwork. Thompson cast a sharp glance around the room, ensuring no one missed a beat. They had practiced this scenario countless times, and now it was real.

Minutes passed, tense and slow. The enemy sub came closer, then passed, unaware of the Defender lurking silently in the deep. As soon as it was clear, Ortiz exhaled.

"Team, well done," she said, her voice filled with pride.

Thompson added, "Mistakes happen, but correcting them fast is how we succeed. We rely on each other down here, and today, we did it right."

The crew exchanged glances of quiet satisfaction. We had faced a challenge together and come out stronger, our bond as a team even tighter than before.

You may not find yourself in a life-or-death situation such as the one I just described, but the tactics employed from *The Character Blueprint* are relevant for any tense situation. As a leader navigating the intricate web of team dynamics, it's crucial to employ strategic approaches in advance of challenges. Practice your roles and reactions, so you and your people are ready to meet the moment when a difficulty or crisis arrives.

Imagine your mission as providing a beacon guiding the team through uncharted waters. It's not enough to merely point in a direction, the path must be illuminated with clarity and precision. Each team member should grasp their task's intricacies, from its overarching goals to the minute details of execution. By envisioning the journey ahead, leaders set the stage for focused, purposeful action.

While following *The Character Blueprint* to define a mission, certain elements must come into play:

- Explain the precise time period for upcoming projects
- Explain in steps how the task should be carried out
- Emphasize the deadline

Considering your leadership mission another way, think of yourself as a skilled conductor assembling a symphony orchestra. Leaders must carefully allocate roles to team members based on their unique strengths and capabilities. It's about creating a harmonious blend of talents, where everyone contributes their distinct notes to the music's melody. By leveraging the full spectrum of skills within the team, leaders ensure that every aspect of the mission is approached with precision and excellence.

Additionally, setting flexible yet achievable deadlines is paramount. Imposing unrealistic targets only serves to heap unnecessary pressure on individuals, potentially compromising the quality of their work. By establishing timelines that strike a balance between ambition and attainability, leaders create an environment where team members can excel without feeling overwhelmed by undue stress.

A collaborative culture promotes an environment where communication is as easy as breathing. Whether it is the ability to share one's opinions, to discuss someone's work quality, or even voicing appreciation for another person, all forms of respectful expression are encouraged. This minimizes any communication gaps, making blunders less likely to occur.

The best way to keep communication flowing smoothly is by scheduling regular follow-ups throughout work processes. Keeping track of problems and achievements gives people an opportunity to share what's on their mind, while measuring progress.

As a leader, it is your responsibility to guide the team by your example. When taking up a task, you should follow the schedule and perform your role according to defined procedures, while reporting throughout the process. Team members will follow what they see more than what you say.

Honest feedback regarding the progress of the team must be provided to people. It's been shown that leadership commentary works—individuals tend to learn from their mistakes and work to improve them, based on constructive critiques. When feedback is lacking, or even if feedback arrives late, it is not possible to improve the work quality. However, it is important to define what honest feedback that produces positive results looks like.

Honest feedback:

- Avoids false flattery for a task a person has performed.
- Politely calls out mistakes and lets a person claim accountability.
- Praises good work.
- Does not pressurize beyond limits.
- If there is any room for improvement, encourages it by setting clear expectations.

Thus, it is important to conduct work in a collaborative way that promotes individuals' creative and innovative mindsets and presents them with an opportunity to showcase their skills best. Team members tend to feel content in leadership reliance and work to achieve the goals dictated to them.

When all roles are clearly assigned and members are encouraged to work in flawless order, with good communication techniques in practice, the odds of accomplishing targeted missions stay high. When there are issues, accountability measures are also easier to pursue.

Accountability and more efficient productivity are possible through using these techniques:

Setting Clear Goals and Expectations

It is important that when roles are assigned based on skills, expected outcomes take human nature into consideration. Even if a person excels at certain skills, they are still likely to make an occasional error or fail at a task. *The Character Blueprint* calls for professionalism versus embarrassing people. A strong leader deals with blunders calmly.

It's acceptable to have a healthy number of expectations for the individuals you lead within the various roles you have assigned them. But if a person is tasked with something entirely different than their usual roles, allow them more flexibility and give them a dose of extra grace.

We have discussed before the importance of teamwork for improved quality of work. But teamwork also enhances innovation in the projects.

Innovation Through Teamwork

We know *great* minds think alike, but we also know that not all minds share the same perspectives. What one person may notice, another person might not. Some people are great at reading between the lines, while others are great at extracting information using different means.

The reason why teams work is because the different skill sets of people are combined for a greater purpose and organizational success. An individual can't perform as well as the team does. No matter how creative one person is, their skills combined and fueled by other creative skills produce a better outcome and lead to innovation. Innovation further leads to new ideas where imagination takes shape and becomes something literal. This promotes a new and exciting dynamic for any business or organization.

Insights From an Old Salt

My experience at one organization stands out. No matter the individual contributions, overall performance consistently fell short of expectations. Each department boasted highly knowledgeable personnel, yet collaboration remained elusive. Impenetrable walls seemed to separate teams, hindering unified action. As a result, enthusiasm waned, and quarterly numbers reflected a downward trend. It became painfully clear: change was imperative.

We soon recognized that our issues originated from very common and basic areas that haunt many businesses.

Transforming a work environment where employees operate in silos (limited and sometimes restrictive communication and collaboration based on a narrowed focus) requires a concerted effort to break down barriers and foster a culture of cooperation and teamwork. Here's a step-by-step guide on how to achieve this:

1. Leadership Commitment: The first step is securing senior leadership buy-in. Leaders must recognize the harm silos inflict on the organization and commit to initiating collaboration. By communicating its importance as a core value, they set the tone for a more cooperative work environment.

2. Communication Channels: Establish clear and open communication channels across departments. Encourage regular meetings, both formal and informal, where teams can share updates, discuss challenges, and align their goals. Utilizing digital collaboration tools such as project management software, messaging platforms, and shared document repositories to facilitate communication and information sharing has proven beneficial.

3. Cross-functional Teams: Create cross-functional teams to tackle projects and initiatives that require input from multiple departments. By bringing together employees with diverse perspectives and expertise, these teams can break down silos and drive innovation. Assign clear roles and responsibilities to team members and empower them to collaborate effectively toward common objectives.

4. Shared Goals and Objectives: Align goals and objectives across departments to promote a sense of unity and shared purpose. Ensure that everyone understands how their contributions support the organization's overarching goals. Encourage collaboration by rewarding teams that work together to achieve shared outcomes rather than solely focusing on individual achievements.

5. Training and Development: Provide training and development opportunities that promote collaboration and interpersonal skills. Offer workshops on effective communication, conflict resolution training, and teamwork resources to equip employees with the tools they need to work collaboratively across departments. Encourage a growth mindset where employees are open to learning from each other and adapting to new ways of getting the job done.

6. Leadership Support and Role Modeling: Leaders play a crucial role in shaping organizational culture. Owners, board of directors, presidents, vice-presidents, managers, supervisors, and the like who demonstrate collaborative behaviors and actively participate in cross-functional initiatives, forge a path their people will follow. Recognizing and rewarding employees who exemplify collaboration and teamwork also reinforces the importance of these values throughout the organization.

7. Feedback Mechanisms: Establish feedback mechanisms to solicit input from employees on how to improve collaboration and teamwork. Encourage open and honest communication and be receptive to suggestions for enhancing cross-departmental collaboration. Act on feedback by implementing changes that address identified issues and barriers to collaboration.

8. Celebrate Successes: Celebrate successes and milestones achieved through collaboration. Recognize teams and individuals who contribute to cross-functional projects and initiatives, highlighting the positive impact of working together toward common goals. By celebrating successes, you reinforce the value of collaboration and inspire others to embrace a cooperative mindset.

9. Continuous Improvement: Collaboration is an ongoing process that requires continuous effort and improvement. Regularly evaluate the effectiveness of collaboration initiatives and make adjustments as needed. Solicit feedback from employees on what is working well and where there is room for improvement and iterate on your approach accordingly.

In my case, by following these steps and encouraging a culture of collaboration, we were able to break down our silos and create a more cohesive and productive work environment. As a result, our employees became more productive, achieved more wins, and obviously enjoyed their work more. And the organization as a whole achieved greater success.

SILOS
BREAKING THROUGH THE BARRIERS
1. LEADERSHIP BUY-IN
Leaders must acknowledge the detrimental effects of silos on the organization and commit to fostering a more collaborative work environment.
2. OPEN COMMUNICATION
Creating clear and open interdepartmental channels of communication branching out from each team to each of the other teams in the organization.
3. EMPOWER DIVERSE TEAMS
Bringing together individuals with diverse background and training allow us to create more effective project teams that break down silos and continue to push innovation.
4. ALIGNMENT OF GOALS
Ensure each departments goals are in alignment with the organizational goals and promote a sense of unity and a shared purpose. Ensure each individual understands how they contribute to
5. TRAINING AND DEVELOPMENT
Seek out training and development opportunities that promote collaboration and interpersonal skills. Encourage an environment where employees are open to learning from each other and adapting to new ways of working.
6. LEAD BY EXAMPLE
Leaders are the forefront of change. By promoting collaborative behaviors and actively participating in cross-functional initiatives, leaders become the example to emulate.
7. CONTINUOUS FEEDBACK
Feedback is essential for individuals and organizations to identify strengths, areas for improvement, and opportunities for growth, fostering continuous learning and development.
8. CELEBRATE SUCCESSES
Take time to recognize and celebrate successes and milestones achieved. This reinforces the value of collaboration and inspire others to embrace a collaborative mindset.
9. CONTINUOUS IMPROVEMENT
Collaboration is more than a one and done, it is an ongoing process that requires continuous effort for improvement. Routinely evaluate effectiveness and make necessary adjustments as needed. Feedback from the team is crucial to continuously improving.
WWW.SUCCESSTHROUGHSELF.COM

Chapter 8: Conflict Resolution and Effective Problem-solving

Conflict is an inevitable aspect of human interaction, especially in teams made up of human beings with contrasting personalities working toward shared goals. However, conflict does not have to be a destructive force. In fact, when addressed with the right approach, conflict can stimulate innovation, strengthen relationships, and steer progress. The key lies in addressing conflict constructively rather than avoiding it altogether.

Consider a team working on a high-stakes project with tight deadlines. Marketing and operations find themselves at odds—marketing wants to push for a bold, high-budget campaign, while operations feel the budget should be allocated more conservatively due to logistical constraints. As tensions rise, a crisis looms. Without a resolution, frustration and mistrust begin to undermine productivity. I like how a former U.S. president approached the topic.

"Peace is not absence of conflict, it is the ability to handle conflict by peaceful means."

-Ronald Reagan

As a leader, your role is to guide the team through conflict. Helping people find solutions that align with overall goals and maintain team cohesion despite differences of opinion is critical to achieving success. This chapter explores proven methods for resolving conflicts effectively and turning challenging moments into opportunities for growth. Leaders who follow *The Character Blueprint* understand that to bring opposing parties into a place of alignment, where they can make forward progress together, it is crucial to first identify the underlying source of their disagreements. By understanding the real root causes of discord, you can better apply appropriate strategies for resolution.

In my experience as a naval leader and trainer, I have found that conflict typically arises from different perspectives, values, or communication styles. Here are some of the most common sources of workplace conflict:

1. **Interpersonal Differences**: Conflicts between individuals based on personality, working style, or communication preferences.

2. **Resource Competition**: Disagreements over limited resources, such as time, budget, or staff.

3. **Goal Misalignment**: Conflicting priorities or objectives between departments or team members.

Understanding which of these root causes sparked a dispute is essential for settling it constructively. In the course of analysis, *The Character Blueprint* reminds leaders that addressing interpersonal issues requires the use of emotional intelligence. Resource and goal conflicts will require a more strategic and problem-solving approach.

Picture a scenario in your workplace where divergent viewpoints clash, threatening to halt progress. If members devolve into right-fighting, raised voices, or refusal to cooperate, the project and perhaps even jobs may be lost. In such moments where the environment could turn volatile without intervention, an objective and professional leader is critical. He or she will model, as well as teach, open communication for conflict resolution by keeping a cool and calm head, as well as a listening ear. Through the implementation of tools and techniques designed to help people reach consensus or come to agreements, teams can transform discord into unity, ensuring that each voice is heard and challenges are met head-on.

The Character Blueprint

Conflict Resolution Framework

When a problem arises, it is vital to remember that everyone is on the same team. This may sound simple, and you may instinctually think, *of course, we all know that.* However, when circumstances do not go as expected or planned, people commonly turn on each other. It's pure human nature—even if we don't mean to or realize what we're doing.

There will be instances when an issue causes major tension in the team disrupting the working environment. This could be due to many things, but regardless of the problematic catalyst, effective conflict resolution can be broken down into a simple, repeatable process. When disagreements occur, follow this four-step framework to guide your team toward a solution. With each step, I've provided an example situation for you to consider.

1. **Identify the Root Cause:** At the first hint of dissension between team members, start by striving to understand the core issue. Often, the apparent conflict is just a surface scratch of a deeper problem. Ask open-ended questions such as, "What do you think is at the heart of the disagreement?" or "What is the outcome you want from this conversation?" This step will help you uncover the true source of tension.

Imagine you are leading a team of software engineers, and two team members are in a heated argument over the coding structure of a new application. Instead of letting the debate become personal, ask each person to articulate their primary concerns about the project and the goals they're trying to achieve. By keeping them keyed in on the work, it's more likely the engineers will realize that while they disagree on the method, they share a common goal: improving the application's efficiency.

2. **Acknowledge Emotions:** Often, conflict involves emotional reactions that can cloud judgment. Acknowledge the passions at play without letting them derail the conversation. Express understanding of feelings like frustration or anxiety and affirm that these emotions are valid.

In a healthcare setting, nurses were upset by a change in shift scheduling. Instead of ignoring the tension, the department leader took the time to meet with each nurse individually in an effort to understand their concerns. By giving them personalized attention and acknowledging their frustrations, the leader defused the situation. They worked resourcefully to create a schedule that worked for everyone.

3. **Collaborate on Solutions:** Once everyone's concerns have been aired, work together to find a resolution that balances competing interests. Encourage open brainstorming and keep the focus on the shared goal, rather than individual agendas.

In a retail company, the marketing and sales departments were at odds over campaign budgets. The marketing team wanted to allocate more resources to online ads, while sales wanted more in-store promotions. The leader facilitated a meeting where both teams presented their needs and challenges. They next guided the group into a brainstorming interval, with growth as a topic, but they emphasized creativity and team spirit over restrictive thinking. By focusing on the shared goal of increasing sales, the team devised a phased strategy that included both online and in-store efforts, optimizing budget allocation while meeting both teams' needs.

4. **Follow-Up:** Once a resolution is reached, ensure that actions are implemented and effective. Schedule follow-up meetings to assess the progress of the solution, check in with those involved, and make adjustments if necessary. This step ensures that the resolution is sustainable and that the team continues to move forward.

A manufacturing company faced persistent tension between its engineering and production teams. The engineering team felt that production was not following the designed processes, while the production team felt the designs were unrealistic. After the leadership team facilitated a solution, they scheduled monthly meetings to review process improvements and provide feedback. Over time, both teams collaborated more effectively, and production delays decreased.

Tools and Techniques for Effective Conflict Resolution

1. **Mediation Techniques**: When conflicts escalate beyond team discussions, a neutral third party can help mediate the situation. A mediator can be someone from outside the team—such as a consultant, coach, or human resource professional—or a respected individual within the group who can facilitate the conversation impartially. *The Character Blueprint* involves effective mediation, ensuring each party has an opportunity to express their concerns and is guided toward a mutually agreeable solution.

2. **De-escalation Phrases**: *The Character Blueprint* uses calming language during conflict that can help prevent escalation and keep the conversation productive. Phrases like:

- "Help me understand your perspective."
- "I see your point, and I think we can work together to address this."
- "Let's focus on the solution rather than the problem."

These phrases shift the conversation from confrontation to collaboration and ensure that all parties feel heard and valued.

Practical Tools/Exercises

1. **Conflict Mapping Exercise**: Part of *The Character Blueprint* process is to identify a past conflict that occurred

within your team. Use the following questions to map out the issue:

- What was the root cause of the conflict?
- What human emotions were involved, and how were they addressed?
- What was the solution, and how did the team collaborate to reach it?
- How did you follow up to ensure the solution was effective?

Reflect on this exercise and identify areas for improvement in your current conflict resolution approach.

2. **Role-Playing Scenarios**: Another diagram in *The Character Blueprint* design is to use role-playing as a training tool, so you can practice conflict resolution techniques. Set up a scenario where team members act out different parts, such as a team leader, an upset employee, and a neutral mediator. After the role-play, discuss what worked well, what didn't, and how the conflict could be resolved more effectively in real life.

Developing Problem-solving Skills

Enhancing problem-solving skills within a team is a multifaceted endeavor that involves promoting the right mindset, providing essential tools, and nurturing a supportive environment. To achieve this, organizations can implement a range of strategies that work in tandem to cultivate a culture of cooperation and innovation. At the core of this approach is *The Character Blueprint,* where the establishment of a collaborative culture, trust, open communication, and mutual respect form the foundation.

Complementary to cultivating a collaborative culture is the role of training and workshops in developing problem-solving and critical thinking skills. These structured environments offer opportunities for individuals to acquire new mastery, knowledge, and perspectives through interactive exercises, tackling real-life situations, and undertaking hands-on tasks. Guided practice and feedback enable participants to analyze problems effectively, identify underlying causes, and develop innovative solutions. Moreover, workshops seed a culture of continuous learning and open-mindedness, empowering participants to approach future challenges with analytical and creative mindsets as a matter of practice. The exchange of ideas among peers during these sessions often leads to the development of assorted strategies and approaches to problem-solving.

Exercises such as *Root Cause Analysis* and *S.W.O.T. Analysis* provide systematic frameworks for structured problem-solving. *Root Cause Analysis* delves into the underlying sources of setbacks, enabling organizations to address core issues rather than just symptoms. Techniques like the *5 Whys* or *Fishbone Diagram* can be employed to identify catalyst causes effectively. *S.W.O.T. Analysis* offers a strategic overview by evaluating an organization's internal strengths and weaknesses, as well as external opportunities and threats. This dual approach stimulates informed decision-making and strategic planning, ensuring that solutions are constructive in the short term and aligned with broader organizational goals.

Encouraging experimentation and innovation, as well as brainstorming sessions, will make critical thinking and problem-solving a healthy habit in your organization. These practices allow employees to explore a variety of ideas without fear of failure, stimulating creative concepts and collaboration. Brainstorming sessions provide a structured yet flexible platform for team members to share and challenge ideas, refining them through collective input. Such processes not only enhance individual analytical skills but also build a resilient, adaptable think-tank capable of tackling complex issues with innovative approaches.

Mentorship programs and cross-functional teams further enhance problem-solving skills by cultivating differing perspectives and collaborative learning. Mentorship programs pair less experienced employees with seasoned mentors, facilitating knowledge transfer and promoting a culture of continuous learning and feedback. Cross-functional teams bring together various skill sets, experiences, and viewpoints, encouraging innovative solutions to complex problems. This diversity broadens the range of potential solutions and enhances critical thinking and adaptive problem-solving abilities.

Technology and tools play a crucial role in enhancing problem-solving by streamlining processes, improving efficiency, and facilitating better communication and collaboration. Advanced software and automation tools handle repetitive tasks, freeing employees to focus on more complex issues. Data analytics tools provide insights for informed decision-making, while project management software ensures tasks are organized and meeting deadlines are met. Collaborative platforms enable seamless teamwork since multiple people can make updates, write notes, and upload documents on a project or for multiple projects, encouraging innovation and idea sharing. Project management software is particularly beneficial for confronting larger scale ventures when a team effort is required.

Creating a safe environment for failure and reframing it as a learning opportunity cultivates a workplace culture where employees feel empowered to take risks and experiment without fear of repercussions. This mindset encourages employees to explore new ideas and approaches. By viewing setbacks as valuable lessons, organizations can harness the collective intelligence of their teams to tackle challenges with resilience and adaptability.

Simulation exercises and real-world problem-solving provide hands-on experience in a safe environment for employees to explore solutions. Simulations offer a controlled setting for experimentation and learning from mistakes. Tackling real-world problems encourages the application of theoretical knowledge to practical scenarios, boosting critical thinking and innovation.

By collecting feedback from various sources, teams can identify areas for enhancement and iterate on their solutions accordingly. Documenting feedback will contribute to a catalogue of best processes and practices, not only explaining what and how you approach tasks, but shedding light on why.

Acknowledging efforts and celebrating successes in the workplace makes people feel recognized and appreciated. It's the kind of atmosphere that motivates employees to actively engage in problem-solving endeavors. A cycle of acknowledgment and celebration creates a supportive environment where innovation flourishes, collaboration thrives, and obstacles are tackled with enthusiasm and determination. *The Character Blueprint* integrates these practices into the team's routine, where problem-solving skills are significantly enhanced, leading to more exciting and profitable solutions.

Insights From an Old Salt

The submarine was preparing to deploy the following day for a critical mission to map the ocean floor topography. But, during the pre-deployment checks, a crucial piece of equipment malfunctioned. The equipment in question was a vital component of the submarine's propulsion system—without which the vessel could not safely operate.

Upon discovering the malfunction, the chain of command convened to determine the course of action. The Leading Chief Petty Officer, Chief, in charge of the equipment, recommended a four-day full repair, stating that any temporary fixes could compromise the safety of the submarine and its crew during the mission. Under pressure to meet deployment deadlines, the Engineering Officer, Engineer suggested a quick patch-up job that would allow the submarine to get underway on time.

Unfortunately, instead of applying effective conflict resolution techniques, tensions continued to rise. The unclear resolution efforts and failure to facilitate open communication between the two leaders only made the situation worse.

As a result, valuable time was wasted in heated debates, and the submarine's departure was unnecessarily delayed. The missed deadline not only reflected poor conflict resolution techniques on the part of leadership, but also a poor understanding of the resources available to the submarine. Hindsight is always 20/20, but a more effective approach to problem-solving and conflict resolution could have been employed. Adhering to the following leadership steps from *The Character Blueprint* would have helped.

1. Established a clear communication channel. Leadership could have encouraged open dialogue and actively listened to understand each party's concerns and perspectives.

2. Sought input from subject matter experts. Leadership could have consulted with experienced engineers and technicians to assess the severity of the equipment malfunction and explored potential solutions.

3. Utilized collaborative problem-solving. Leadership could have encouraged brainstorming sessions to explore alternative approaches that balanced safety considerations with mission objectives.

4. Made decisions based on consensus. Leadership could have strived to reach a consensus among the chain of command, acknowledging the importance of both safety and mission readiness.

By applying these conflict resolution and problem-solving techniques effectively, the submarine's departure could have been expedited without compromising the safety of the crew or the success of the mission.

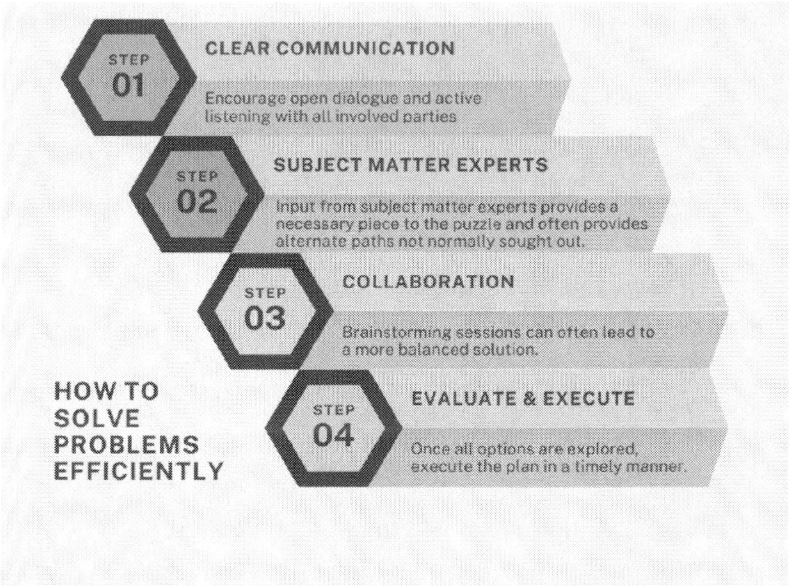

Chapter 9: Leading with Character

Leadership is not static; it is full of ongoing shifts and turns, much like an ever-evolving river that continuously adapts and reconfigures its course. The flow of character in leadership is dynamic, formed by experiences, decisions, and personal growth. Great leaders inspire through their actions, integrity, and authenticity. Think about the leaders who have had the most significant impact on your life. What sets them apart? Likely, it's their character—how they treat others, make decisions, and remain true to their values, especially under pressure. Leadership begins with personal character, and that character shapes the success of the entire team, just as a river molds the landscape.

Developing strong character is not a one-time effort—it is a continuous process that requires ongoing intentionality and reflection. That's why *The Character Blueprint* serves as a guide to help you instill the leadership qualities that define not only your own success but also the success of those around you.

The Foundations of Character in Leadership

Character is the bedrock upon which trust, respect, and capable guidance are built. Cultivating the following traits is essential to inspiring and motivating people, while creating a positive work environment that drives sustainable success. Just remember, these traits are not fixed; they are ever evolving.

- **Integrity** is the steady current of leadership, guiding every decision and action. It's the foundation that keeps leaders grounded, no matter how turbulent the waters. In addition to being honest, having strong moral principles, and doing the right thing—even when it's difficult, integrity means keeping commitments. Just as a river cannot flow without a current pushing it, leadership cannot thrive without integrity's drive.

Real-World Example: During a financial crisis at a small company, the CEO took a significant pay cut to avoid laying off employees. By prioritizing the well-being of his team over personal financial gain, and proving his commitment to his people, this leader demonstrated integrity. His transparency and dedication inspired deep loyalty throughout the business. Just as a river nourishes the land it passes through a leader who follows *The Character Blueprint* nurtures the people under their care.

Character Challenge: Think of a recent situation where you had to make a tough decision. Did your actions align with your values? How can you ensure that your integrity remains an unbroken current in every aspect of your leadership?

- **Empathy** is the flow that forges connections between people. A leader who understands and cares about the needs and emotions of others strengthens teamwork and trust. Like water moving through a riverbed, empathy adapts to the needs of those it touches, forming deep, supportive bonds in the trenches.

Real-World Example: While managing a team on a critical project with a tight deadline, a manufacturing leader noticed signs of burnout. Rather than pushing the team harder with the promise of "we'll make it up to you later," she acknowledged their efforts and offered support. This wise leader provided options that promoted a healthier work-life balance, such as adjusting workloads or flexible hours. While adjusting deadlines was not always feasible, she considered it as a solution when possible. Demonstrating empathy in this way led to improved morale and sustained productivity, helping the team stay motivated and focused even under pressure.

Character Challenge: For the next week, actively practice empathy by checking in with at least one team member each day to ask how they are doing—personally and professionally. Take time to listen without offering advice or solutions. Reflect afterwards, asking yourself, *how did this impact my relationship with each person? Did it change the flow of communication within our team?*

- **Vision** is like a river that has found its path. It gives direction—not only for the present but also for the future. Visionary leaders help their teams see beyond current objectives or day-to-day operations, inspiring people to play a role in something larger than themselves. Just as every river carves out its own unique course, each leader's vision sculpts the direction of their team's collective efforts.

Real-World Example: The founders of a tech company had a bold vision to transform archaic paper correspondence into an efficient information flow using digital techniques. By clearly articulating this vision and aligning team efforts, the founders motivated employees to think imaginatively and renovate. This resulted in groundbreaking products that positioned the company as an industry leader.

Character Challenge: Consider your focus. Are you targeting the future as well as the present? Are you tasking those you lead to keep their eyes on the bigger picture, while they simultaneously tackle your current goals and objectives? Surround yourself and others with reminders about the importance of paying attention to both the daily details *and* your overall vision.

- **Humility** is like a river source that that feeds the waters flowing downstream. It allows leaders to recognize that their primary emphasis needs to be about serving others, not making themselves look good or important. A humble leader values the contributions of all team members and remains open to learning and growth. Like the invisible nutrients held inside each trickle of water, humility feeds others, letting them flourish, rise, and shine.

Real-World Example: In a team meeting, an employee presented an idea that challenged the leader's long-standing approach. Though the leader felt an emotional sting, instead of dismissing the employee's suggestion, he thanked them for the insight. After the meeting, the leader invested time and energy thoughtfully considering the proposal. This meant meeting with the employee to ask additional questions and discuss the matter further. Going through the process with an inquisitive mind and humble heart not only strengthened the leader's relationship with that employee but also launched a culture of innovation and openness.

Character Challenge: Review your responses when a situation triggers your emotions. Do you respond defensively or are you able to maintain composure in a way that keeps your ears open, so you listen to hear with a curious mind? Are you overly protective and possessive of ideas, projects, innovations, processes, etc., or do you share info and accept suggestions freely? Do you consider the opinions, judgements, plans, innovations, concepts, proposals, etc. others offer, or do you shut down any idea that isn't your own? If your honest gut-check feels uncomfortable or you know the truth hits farther from the humility target than you'd like, commit to taking a humble leadership approach starting today.

Character-driven leaders hold themselves accountable for their actions and decisions. They take responsibility for both successes and failures, setting a powerful example for their people. This accountability encourages an environment of ownership and continuous improvement, where everyone strives to do their best and learn from mistakes.

The Positive Effects of Leading with *The Character Blueprint*

Leading with character produces numerous positive outcomes for both individuals and organizations. When leaders demonstrate strong character, employees are more likely to feel engaged and motivated. Character-driven leadership promotes a sense of purpose and dedication within teams. Just as a river inspires growth along its banks, leadership rooted in integrity, empathy, vision, and humility encourages employees to align their personal values with the organization's mission. This alignment propels them to go above and beyond in their roles, creating a powerful current of motivation that drives everyone forward.

Character-driven leadership also profoundly impacts the organizational atmosphere. It creates an environment of transparency, respect, and partnership. Leaders who demonstrate integrity, empathy, vision, and humility encourage employees to share original ideas and cooperate openly. This kind of environment attracts top talent and increases retention of existing employees, thus reducing turnover and its associated costs.

Additionally, leaders with strong character make decisions based on proven principles, factual data, and ethical considerations. Like a river's steady flow, they prioritize long-term benefits over short-term gains, carefully considering the impact of their choices on all stakeholders. This approach nurtures responsible decision-making, benefiting the organization, its employees, and society as a whole, much like a river's enrichment of the ecosystems it flows through.

Satya Nadella's leadership at Microsoft provides an excellent example of how character-driven leadership yields positive outcomes. When Nadella became CEO, he prioritized empathy and a growth mindset, significantly reshaping Microsoft's philosophy. His leadership encouraged teamwork, trust, and originality, transforming Microsoft into a leading tech company and creating an environment where employees felt valued and motivated. Nadella's character-driven approach revitalized the company.

I can't imagine it was easy for Nadella, especially during the early months of leadership transition. He must have felt tempted and tested when managing teams that faced tight deadlines. But from all reports, rather than intensifying the pressure on people, he acknowledged their hard work and offered support, such as flexible work hours and regular check-ins to ensure they had what they needed. I've thought about how this shift in leadership approach affected team morale. I'm sure some initially felt confused, others might have been downright skeptical or paranoid. But over time, Nadella won them over with his adherence to traits you find in *The Character Blueprint.*

If someone were to study your leadership methods or to write your story based on employee interviews, what would those reports say? If you dare, I have another Character Challenge for you. Over the next week, actively reflect on how your actions align with your core values. Consider how your leadership behaviors impact your team's engagement and morale. Are you nurturing an environment of openness, partnership, and trust that produces the results you want?

If your honest answer is no, remember, the best time to start following *The Character Blueprint* is at the beginning of your leadership journey. The second-best time is now!

The Difficulties of Leading with Character

While leading with character offers immense benefits, it's not without its challenges. Like a river encountering obstacles in its path, leaders face difficulties that test their resolve and commitment to their values.

- **Ethical Dilemmas:** Like a river encountering a fork in its path, leaders must weigh competing interests, consider potential consequences, and make decisions that align with their values and goals. One of the most significant challenges a leader faces is navigating ethical dilemmas. These situations often involve complex decisions where the right course of action isn't always clear. Maintaining ethical leadership while balancing the needs of various stakeholders is difficult, especially when external pressures push for short-term results.

Real-World Example: A stark example of failing to lead with character is seen in the Enron scandal, revealed in the early 2000s. The company's leaders compromised their integrity for short-term financial gain, ultimately leading to the company's collapse. Not only did thousands of employees lose their jobs, benefits, and retirement accounts, but people all over the world lost their capital investments totaling in the billions. Enron literally created a global economic earthquake. This illustrates how a lack of ethical leadership can have devastating consequences, emphasizing the importance of staying true to core principles in the face of external pressures—regardless of the temptation.

Character Challenge: There's a saying that is scary but true: "We don't keep secrets. Secrets keep us." Write down the core principles that keep consciences clean, allow people to sleep without guilt or regret at night, and ensure that your reputation and that of your family name are respected and respectable. Keep this list of principles close at hand for regular review to remind you of your commitment to character and why you are resolved to adhering to *The Character Blueprint.*

- **Consistency in Decision-Making:** Consistency is key to building trust, but under pressure, it can be challenging to maintain. Leaders often face conflicting demands, and staying true to one's principles requires resilience. Leaders must hold firm to their values, even when compromising seems easier. Otherwise, just as a river that expands beyond its banks creates chaos and damage, so a flood of emotions can leave a path of destruction in an inconsistent leader's wake.

Real-World Example: Though he had been a mid-level manager in the financial industry for several years, Bill felt stuck. He couldn't understand why he was continuously passed over for promotions. He also struggled with chronic personnel problems that wouldn't go away. He constantly found himself thinking, *if only my people would listen to me and do their job, I wouldn't be so stressed all the time.* What Bill failed to realize was that he often confused people by changing priorities, giving conflicting directives, or saying one thing but claiming he said the opposite a short time later. Behind his back, it was regularly said of Bill, "Be careful when he tells you something, because he constantly changes the rules in the middle of the game—especially if it means he will make you lose so he can win."

Character Challenge: Reflect on a recent leadership challenge where your values were tested. Did external pressures influence your decision-making? What constants guide your decisions in a congruent way? Do your people view you as a leader who communicates clearly, concisely, and consistently? Do they know what you expect and why? Do your team members believe your decisions are made for the greatest good versus for your personal gain? How can you ensure the accuracy of your answers? Follow due-diligence practices and investigate to find the truth.

Strategies for Overcoming Challenges

Although the challenges of leading with character can seem daunting, there are several strategies leaders can use to overcome obstacles and stay true to their intrinsic standards. Like a river that adapts to changes in the landscape, leaders must be flexible, self-aware, and committed to their principles.

- **Self-awareness** is fundamental to character-driven leadership. Regular reflection on one's values and actions ensure alignment with principles. Leaders must stay mindful of their growth opportunities, strengths, and weaknesses, making intentional choices that reinforce their character.

- **Seek Mentorship and Support:** No leader navigates challenges alone. Seeking guidance from mentors, peers, or professional networks provides valuable perspectives. These objective viewpoints provide additional resources and support, helping leaders stay true to their character.

- **Open Communication:** Maintaining open lines of communication is essential for efficiency, accuracy, resolving conflicts, and managing criticism. Leaders should create an atmosphere of active listening, empathy, and transparency, ensuring all voices are heard. Communication must be responsive and continuous.

- **Ethical Decision-Making:** Leaders should prioritize ethics in every decision. Establishing clear principles that guide actions, considering long-term consequences, and consulting diverse stakeholders helps leaders navigate challenges with integrity. Leaders who prioritize ethics maintain a steady course.

- **Resilience:** Resilient leaders develop coping strategies, practice self-care, and maintain a positive outlook even in the face of adversity. Resilient leaders stay focused on their long-term goals, overcoming obstacles and emerging stronger through challenges.

How to Build an Environment That Develops Leaders

To foster a workplace where leadership thrives, organizations must cultivate a setting where individuals are empowered to take ownership and grow. The following list should be prioritized by every leader whose goal is to produce lasting results.

1. **Set Clear Expectations**
2. **Empower Team Members**
3. **Provide Learning Opportunities**
4. **Encourage Constructive Feedback**
5. **Support Innovation**
6. **Lead by Example**
7. **Promote Resilience**
8. **Create Networking Opportunities**

Consider your organization's culture.

- Are there opportunities for individuals to step up as leaders?

- Is *The Character Blueprint* part of the information and educational process for new leaders?

- When leaders face a challenge, do they know to stay true to your core principles and to follow the success strategies we've covered to guide their decisions?

- Does every leader in your organization have access to the priority list above, understanding that implementing it into their daily practices will produce lasting results?

Navigating the ongoing shifts and turns of leadership becomes easier when you follow *The Character Blueprint* map. You may not know exactly what's coming around the bend, but with good guidance, you never have to go into it blind.

Insights From an Old Salt

Imagine a team struggling with a longstanding culture of dependency and micromanagement, resulting in low morale, high turnover, and stagnation. What was once a promising group has devolved into mere followers, stripped of their autonomy and initiative. Members have settled into a state of resignation and disappointment, their creative suggestions routinely disregarded. They hesitate to act without explicit consent, fearing repercussions, and many find themselves feeling trapped and undervalued. This is not a figment of imagination. The scenario I just described reflects the reality of one of my recent team experiences. Turning this culture around was not easy, but by taking the following steps, I eventually got this team back on its feet.

1. Assessed the Current Culture

The first step in transforming a team culture is to conduct a thorough assessment of its current state. This involves gathering feedback from team members through surveys, interviews, and observation. Identify the core issues: Are employees micromanaged? Is there a lack of communication and transparency? Understanding these problems provided me with a foundation for targeted interventions.

After I gained an understanding of where the team stood, I was able to begin reshaping its future, following *The Character Blueprint.* By identifying core issues and committing to intentional leadership, I worked with others to create an environment where teams thrived.

2. Established a Clear Vision and Core Values

Creating a compelling vision for the future is crucial. This vision should align with the organization's goals and emphasize the importance of leadership development. In this case, we defined core values that supported the organization's vision, such as empowerment, collaboration, innovation, and accountability. These values served as guiding principles throughout the transformation process.

3. **Lead** by **Example**

Leadership transformation starts at the top. Senior leaders and managers must embody the desired values and behaviors they hope to see in their people. I worked hard to demonstrate openness, encourage feedback, and show a willingness to delegate and trust my team. By modeling behaviors found in

The Character Blueprint, I discovered it was easier to inspire our team members to follow suit.

4. Empowered Employees

Empowerment is at the heart of a leadership-oriented culture. With our team, I encouraged employees to take initiative, make decisions, and take ownership of their work. We achieved this by reducing micromanagement and giving team members more autonomy. We provided them with the resources and authority they needed to succeed. This not only built confidence in people but also contributed to a sense of responsibility and accountability.

5. Fostered Open Communication

Create an environment where open and honest communication is encouraged and watch amazing outcomes occur. For our team, I established regular feedback mechanisms, such as one-on-one meetings, team discussions, and anonymous surveys. I ensured that employees felt safe to voice their opinions, ideas, and concerns without fear of retribution. Transparency in communication helped build trust and a sense of community within the team.

6. Promoted Continuous Learning and Development

Investing in the continuous development of employees is crucial for strengthening leadership. We offered training programs, workshops, and seminars that focused on leadership skills, such as strategic thinking, conflict resolution, and emotional intelligence. We encouraged employees to pursue professional development opportunities and provided them with the time and resources to do so.

7. Recognized and Rewarded Leadership Behaviors

Recognition and rewards play a significant role in reinforcing desired behaviors. We made sure we acknowledged and celebrated instances where employees demonstrated exceptional leadership qualities. We used a variety of methods, including formal recognition programs, promotions, or simple gestures of appreciation. Rewarding leadership behaviors motivated others to follow suit and fostered a positive and supportive work environment.

8. Created Opportunities for Growth

Provide opportunities for employees to step into leadership roles and most will exceed your expectations. For our team, we offered people the chance to lead projects, head committees, or mentor newer employees. These experiences helped individuals develop their leadership skills in a practical, hands-on manner. Additionally, these exercises ensured there was a clear path for career advancement within the organization.

9. Built a Collaborative Environment

Encourage teamwork and collaboration for the greater good, then the greatest surprises happen. Changing our culture meant changing mindsets, where team members supported each other and worked together toward common goals. Collaborative environments enabled the sharing of knowledge and ideas, which is essential for innovation and growth. Team-building activities and cross-departmental projects helped strengthen bonds between people, which in turn produced more powerful results.

10. Monitored and Adjusted

Continually monitor the progress of the cultural transformation. Throughout our culture shift, we collected feedback, assessed outcomes, and prepared to make adjustments as necessary. As an ongoing process, I knew it was essential to remain flexible and responsive to the evolving needs of the team and our organization.

LIFE
No Matter
What Happens
WORK
KEEP YOUR BALANCE

Chapter 10: Nurturing Presence and Participation

Strength through unity doesn't fail with grand gestures—it slips through the cracks of everyday moments. A meeting begins. A few familiar voices speak up, dominating the conversation, while the rest fade into the background.

All of the attendees may appear equally qualified, professional, and deserving of their seat at the table, but what happens within the room reveals a deeper truth. Representation without allowing uninhibited participation is an illusion.

This chapter invites you to step into that room—not as a participant, but as an observer—and see what often goes unnoticed. It's a closer look at how leadership choices, however subtle, shape who feels seen, heard, and valued. This in turn determines whether crucial knowledge, information, and wisdom is shared by *everyone* who will be affected by decisions or who will affect those discernments. Missing just one valuable insight could create a cascade of costly consequences.

Leaders guided by *The Character Blueprint* remain steadfast in their resolve to engage the full presence of their people and advance the participation of the entire team. To successfully achieve this and gain the benefit of everyone's input requires careful self-analysis by leaders. There must be no bias allowed to hinder, paralyze, or halt contributions. But exactly what kind of biases are we talking about?

The most commonly called out biases are related to gender and racial prejudices. But there are many other buried roots that create division and exclusion. Some examples include biases based on personality, age, education, title, department someone works in, religious beliefs, political leanings, social stature, hobbies and interests, plus many more we overlook.

Whether male or female, regardless of our skin color or cultural heritage, whether the biases come from the list above or another reason, and coming from any side, a leader can be susceptible to subconscious or even knowingly treating certain people groups differently. A high percentage have an unrecognized pattern of showing favoritism to one while discounting, ignoring, or even making disparaging remarks to or about another.

When this topic is brought up with leaders, the first instinct for most is to deny. However, with honest introspection, the majority confess to making unwarranted judgements, even expressing surprise at the undetected biases they realize they've carried. It is when this is identified and accepted with maturity and wisdom that strong leaders can practice intentionality to make corrections.

Leaders who exemplify the character traits we covered previously: integrity, empathy, vision, and humility, are not afraid to make public apologies to their teams. They commit to leading in a way that invites *all* members to show up, stay present, and participate, with no fear of disregard or hostility. Then from that moment forward, they facilitate meetings based on intentional design. Their eyes, ears, and mind are bent on including each voice, so every person in the room feels seen, heard, and respected.

Character-driven leadership requires recognizing diversity in all its forms—including background, language, and thought—and taking active steps to ensure all are considered. When done well, making it safe for everyone to participate drives innovation, strengthens collaboration, improves communication, and enhances team morale and performance.

A Meeting Observed: When Diversity Isn't Enough

Imagine you're observing a team meeting at a mid-sized tech company—a room filled with talent and potential. The group includes professionals from different cultural backgrounds, gender identities, and experience levels. It's the kind of team that, on paper, reflects a company's commitment to diversity.

The manager begins the meeting by swiftly reviewing the agenda, then immediately turns to their go-to group for input. These individuals—confident, outspoken, and closely aligned with the manager's background—dominate the discussion from the outset. The rest of the team watches as a predictable dynamic unfolds.

One by one, subtle but telling moments surface:

- Sofia, a skilled software engineer with a quiet voice and big ideas, starts to contribute. But before she finishes her first sentence, the manager cuts her off and shifts attention back to the voices they're more comfortable with, unintentionally sidelining her.

- Raj, a seasoned developer, offers a well-thought-out solution to a recurring issue. His idea is met with a brief nod, then dismissed in favor of comments from those already steering the conversation.

- Lena, a junior team member, remains silent. She has fresh, innovative ideas, but past experiences of being told she hasn't been there long enough to "know" has made her feel like her insights have no merit and have conditioned her to hold back.

Throughout the meeting, the body language says what words do not:

- Sofia fidgets with her pen, eyes downcast, visibly withdrawn after the blowoff by their manager.
- Raj leans back, arms crossed—not in defiance, but in quiet resignation.
- Lena avoids eye contact, her posture folded inward.

Despite the detached demeanor of Sofia, Raj, and Lena, the manager closes the meeting with enthusiastic praise—once again for the same select group that has dominated the room. There's no check-in with those who didn't speak, no inquiries made for alternative perspectives. From an external vantage point, the emotional toll is clear: disengagement, disillusionment, and a quiet erosion of psychological safety.

This team may be diverse, but it is not balanced.

Where Good Intentions Fall Short

In today's business landscape, organizations frequently highlight their dedication to valuing their people. Mission statements are updated and training sessions are held. These efforts are well-intended—and necessary—but they are not sufficient.

Inclusion isn't solely about who's in the room. There needs to be emphasis on who feels heard, respected, and empowered to contribute. True character-based leadership requires intention, empathy, and the humility to pause and ask: *Whose voices are missing? Whose ideas aren't being heard?*

A sound strategic plan should include the *lived* experience of your team—who gets to speak, whose ideas are considered, who feels safe to be present and engaged, who is allowed to participate at the highest level? Often, our strategies don't consider who gets left out when conversations move too fast or stay too narrow. Who has something profitable to add, even though they aren't the first or loudest ones to speak?

Building Teams That Include – Not Just Diversify

One of the biggest hurdles for any organization is the ingrained nature of existing cultural norms and power structures that favor the status quo. Leaders must be willing to question the status quo, challenge these norms, and when needed, create spaces where all employees can thrive.

To bridge the gap between policy and practice, businesses need to take intentional steps to set clear expectations for behavior that emphasizes presence and participation. Ongoing training and resources, and actively seeking feedback from employees about their experiences to improve processes should be prioritized. Leaders should model openness and be held accountable for creating and maintaining an accepting environment where all members feel appreciated for their skills, abilities, thoughts, and ideas. Additionally, recognizing and celebrating diverse contributions equally can help reinforce the value of all employees and encourage a more engaged and innovative workforce.

Leadership Scenario: The Project Assignment

You're dividing up a high-visibility project. Without thinking, you assign the technical lead role to someone who's led similar work before—a confident, well-known team member. A junior employee with the right skills, but less visibility, is passed over without consideration.

What to do:

- Pause and reflect. Are you rewarding familiarity over potential?
- Reopen the conversation. Invite others to express interest or share how they'd approach the challenge.
- Build pathways. Consider co-leads or stretch assignments that support growth and collaboration.

Habits of a Character-Driven Leader

Active Listening: Wise leaders prioritize listening to understand diverse perspectives. They give their full attention during conversations, encourage input from all team members, and validate each person's contributions.

Empathy: They practice empathy by putting themselves in others' shoes, recognizing we benefit from understanding different experiences, and responding with compassion and understanding.

Self-awareness: Leaders committed to character regularly reflect on their own biases and behaviors. They do not automatically deny and defend, instead, they seek feedback and are open to learning and growth.

Transparency: They communicate openly and honestly with their teams, sharing information and decisions clearly to build trust and accountability. If they mess up, they are the first to fess up, versus trying to cover up.

Collaboration: Character-driven leaders foster a collaborative environment by encouraging teamwork and ensuring everyone has a chance to contribute to discussions and decision-making processes.

Advocacy: They actively advocate for well-rounded teams made up of people with a variety of differences within the organization, to ensure enriched outcomes. They champion initiatives and policies promoting equity and balance.

Flexibility: Character-committed leaders are adaptable and open to new ideas and approaches. All viable suggestions do not have to come from them. They recognize that different perspectives can lead to innovative solutions.

Mentorship: They provide mentorship and support to all team members, helping them develop their skills and advance their careers.

Recognition: Leaders who follow *The Character Blueprint* celebrate the achievements and contributions of all team members, ensuring that everyone feels valued and appreciated.

Continuous Learning: They commit to ongoing education about caring for their people. They stay informed about best practices and seek out new ways to improve their leadership.

Understanding people and how to inspire their presence and motivate their participation is one of the most important skills any leader can cultivate. If you can accomplish that task, you can achieve nearly anything. Next, I want to paint a picture of a common organizational issue, then offer some questions for you to reflect on. This is the kind of exercise that can help you level up your impact on the people you influence.

Leadership Scenario: Feedback with Bias

After a management performance review discussion, you notice that the feedback for team members is not offered equally. For some, it is more focused on personality ("she's nice," "he needs to be more assertive," "she's too bossy," "he's not friendly enough") while others get feedback tied solely to work outcomes and results.

What to do:

- Raise the issue. Ask your team, *"Are we giving everyone equally actionable feedback?"*

- Guide the shift. Encourage framing feedback around impact, goals, and growth potential. Focus on work-related data not ingrained gender, cultural, or personality expectations.

- Set the tone. Model how to give balanced, constructive feedback in future sessions.

Character Challenge

- When was the last time you made room for someone who doesn't typically speak up?

- How does your meeting structure include or exclude certain voices?

- What one thing can you do this week to model character-driven leadership?

Insights From an Old Salt

In this edition of *Insights from an Old Salt*, I want to share a message I received from one of my colleagues. This message came to me when I first began writing this book and asked for any stories or insights into my leadership style. I am humbled by this perspective.

I remember the day-to-day of being in that office, the feeling of unease was palpable. The team was only focused on meeting the minimum requirements to be able to go home.

Conversations would shift or quiet down when certain members of our leadership entered the room. They were polite enough, but there was this unspoken message that the rest of us didn't quite belong. The few attempts we made to contribute were either ignored or dismissed with a quick nod before they moved on to something else. Our ideas didn't seem to matter, and it didn't take long for us to start doubting ourselves. I kept my head down, did my work, and tried not to make waves.

What made it worse was the leadership at the time. The senior manager seemed more concerned with maintaining the status quo than with making any meaningful changes. I wanted to contribute and be part of the team, but it was hard to trust anyone or even believe that my voice would ever be heard.

When Senior Chief Brooks joined our team, I was skeptical. I'd seen new leaders come and go—each promising change but delivering more of the same. I wasn't about to get my hopes up again. But from the start, something felt different.

He didn't arrive with a grand plan or an authoritative tone. Instead, he led with curiosity and humility. He held one-on-one meetings with each of us—not just as a formality, but to truly listen. When it was my turn, I hesitated. I'd learned to keep my guard up. But he asked thoughtful questions about my experience, my ideas, even my frustrations. And for the first time in a long while, I felt like someone genuinely cared.

He didn't stop at listening. Subtle changes began to take shape. He encouraged broader collaboration, making sure that everyone had space to contribute. Conversations that used to be dominated by a few familiar voices began to shift. My ideas were not only heard—they were discussed and, at times, even implemented. Slowly, I started to lower my defenses.

Then one day, he pulled me aside and said he valued my input—that he saw potential in me. I hadn't heard words like that in years. Suddenly, work felt different. I wasn't just showing up to do a job; I was part of something meaningful. I belonged.

Over the following months, the team dynamic transformed. People opened up—not just about work, but about their lives, their hopes, and their challenges. We learned each other's stories. Inclusion wasn't just a checkbox; it became our culture. I felt more engaged, more willing to speak up, and more invested in our shared success.

I began to believe in his vision, not because it was polished or perfect, but because it was rooted in people. The change wasn't flashy or immediate, but it was real—and lasting.

Looking back, I realize how close I was to disengaging completely. But one leader's choice to lead with empathy and inclusion made all the difference. It showed me that a workplace can be more than just a paycheck. It can be a place where people thrive—where every voice matters, and trust is built through everyday actions.

This story, shared by a colleague, stayed with me—because it's more than a story. It's a mirror. A reminder that leadership isn't about commanding attention or having all the answers. It's about presence. It's about the quiet power of making others feel seen, heard, and valued.

In so many workplaces, it's the quieter voices, the less familiar faces, the untapped perspectives that go unnoticed. Not out of malice, but out of habit. And yet, real leadership begins the moment we choose to break that pattern—to lead not with certainty, but with curiosity and care.

What transformed this team wasn't a bold new strategy or sweeping change. It was something far more powerful: small, intentional acts rooted in empathy. A question asked. A voice elevated. An invitation to participate. A moment of connection that said, *"You matter here."*

To those in leadership—pause for a moment. What kind of space are you creating? One where people feel safe to show up fully, or one where they shrink to fit in? Are you listening deeply, not just to what's said, but to what's left unsaid? Are you nurturing growth in all corners of your team—not just where it's most convenient?

And to every team member reading this: your voice has power. Never underestimate what one moment of courage can do—what one honest conversation, one shared idea, one act of allyship can spark. Change often begins not with a breakthrough, but with a decision—to care, to speak, to try.

In the end, this isn't just a story of one leader or one team. It's a blueprint. A reminder that inclusion is not a box to check—it's a way of showing up, every day. And when we lead with that kind of intention, the impact goes far beyond productivity or performance. We create spaces where people thrive. Where trust grows. Where we rise—together. Where victories occur!

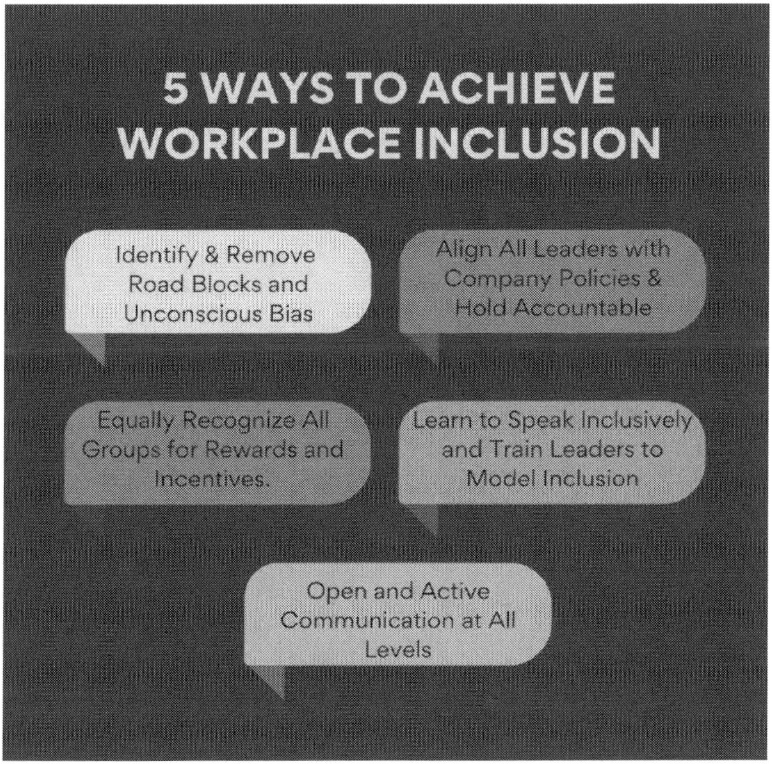
5 WAYS TO ACHIEVE WORKPLACE INCLUSION
Identify & Remove Road Blocks and Unconscious Bias
Align All Leaders with Company Policies & Hold Accountable
Equally Recognize All Groups for Rewards and Incentives.
Learn to Speak Inclusively and Train Leaders to Model Inclusion
Open and Active Communication at All Levels

Chapter 11: Sustaining Character Growth in Teams and Organizations

We've established that building strong character traits is essential for personal growth, professional success, and nurturing positive relationships. Character development often yields rewarding results. However, maintaining consistency presents a significant challenge. Even with a clear understanding of the practices involved, individuals may find themselves deviating from their goals on certain days. While some character traits become ingrained in our personalities, others require continuous practice to solidify. I think the following quote encapsulates the process.

"Perseverance is not a long race; it is many short races one after the other."

-Walter Elliot.

Character development is not a one-time effort but an ongoing resolve requiring dedication and perseverance. It involves a deep understanding of oneself, a commitment to personal values, and the willingness to adapt and grow. This chapter explores the importance of building strong character traits, the challenges faced in maintaining them, and strategies for consistent personal development.

Challenges in Building and Maintaining Character Traits

Despite the clear benefits of strong character traits, maintaining consistency in character development can be challenging. Internal factors such as self-doubt, fear of failure, and lack of motivation can hinder progress. Additionally, external factors such as societal pressures, environmental influences, and unexpected life events can disrupt the development process.

- **Internal Factors:** Self-doubt and fear of failure are significant internal barriers to character development, which in turn, can undermine a leader's ultimate success. Individuals may question their abilities or worry about making mistakes, which can prevent them from fully committing to their goals. For example, someone striving to build integrity may doubt their ability to consistently make ethical decisions, leading to hesitation, avoidance, and lack of motivation. In this instance, making an effort to identify situations that cause doubt, hesitation, or block motivation is the first step in developing confidence and character. Reflecting on one's personal values, reminding yourself *why* you committed to those goals, are next steps to helping break past the internal barriers, so they no longer hold you back.

- **External Factors:** External influences, such as societal expectations and environmental conditions, can also impact character development. For instance, in a highly competitive work environment, employees may feel pressured to cut corners or engage in unethical behavior to achieve targets, undermining their integrity. Additionally, unexpected life events, such as health issues or financial crises, can create stress and distraction, making it difficult to focus on personal growth. A mentor can keep a leader grounded and less susceptible to emotional decisions they may regret later. Creating a culture that values integrity over competition breaks through external barriers. Teams and leaders alike flourish from environments built around "learning from our mistakes." And when ethical behavior expectations are reinforced through policies, training, and leadership examples, the power of external factors diminishes.

Strategies for Developing and Strengthening Character Traits

To overcome these challenges, individuals can adopt various strategies to support their character development journey. One effective approach is to set clear, achievable goals and regularly track progress. This helps maintain focus and motivation, providing a sense of accomplishment as milestones are reached.

Practical techniques such as mindfulness, meditation, and journaling can also support .character development. These practices promote self-awareness and reflection, helping individuals recognize and address negative thoughts and behaviors. For example, mindfulness exercises can help individuals stay present and make conscious choices that align with their values. Journaling allows individuals to document their experiences and reflect on their progress, providing insights into areas for improvement and moments for celebration.

Seeking feedback from trusted friends, family members, or mentors can provide valuable insights and encouragement. Constructive feedback helps individuals understand how their actions are perceived by others and identify areas where they can improve. For instance, a mentor or coach can offer guidance on how to handle ethical dilemmas in the workplace, reinforcing the importance of integrity.

Creating a supportive environment is another crucial factor in maintaining consistency. Surrounding oneself with positive influences, such as like-minded individuals and supportive communities, can reinforce desired traits and behaviors. For example, joining a professional organization that promotes ethical standards can provide ongoing education, resources, and support for maintaining integrity. Organizations can encourage character development in professional settings by promoting integrity, empathy, and resilience.

Self-reflection is a powerful tool for personal growth. Taking time to reflect on one's actions, decisions, and experiences can provide deeper insights into one's character and areas for improvement. Regular self-reflection helps individuals stay aligned with their values and make necessary adjustments to their behavior. For example, reflecting on a challenging situation at work can help an individual identify how they handled the situation, what they learned, and how they can apply those lessons in the future.

Developing a routine that incorporates character-building activities can also support consistency, such as setting aside time each day for envisioning exercises, where you imagine a scenario you are concerned about or want to succeed at, and you see yourself acting exactly as you wish in your mind. Repeating this exercise has been shown to produce a much higher percentage of desired results when the real-life situation occurs. You can also listen to topical podcasts for areas you want to strengthen, such as communication, empathy, humility, courage, etc. Establishing a routine creates a sense of discipline and commitment, making it easier to maintain progress over time.

Implementing Character Development Programs in Organizations

To effectively sustain character growth, organizations should consider implementing structured character development programs. These can include:

Leadership Training

Equip leaders with the skills and knowledge to model and promote strong character traits within their teams. Leaders play a crucial role in shaping organizational culture and setting the tone for behavior, yet most leaders are not educated prior to their roles on how to deal with people effectively. Most leaders get on-the-job training through trial-by-fire. This does them or their people a great disservice. But by providing leaders with targeted training in *Character Blueprint* leadership organizations can ensure that these values are consistently demonstrated from the top down. Leadership training can include workshops, seminars, and ongoing coaching sessions that focus on a leader's ability to inspire and motivate others through exemplary behavior. When leaders embody strong character traits, they set a powerful example for their teams and create an environment where actions match stated missions.

Ethics Workshops

Conduct regular workshops focused on ethical decision-making, integrity, and other key character traits. Ethics workshops provide employees with the tools and knowledge to navigate complex moral dilemmas and make decisions that align with the organization's values. These workshops should be interactive, incorporating real-world scenarios and case studies that challenge participants to think critically and apply ethical principles. Facilitated discussions, role-playing exercises, and group problem-solving activities can help reinforce the importance of integrity, honesty, and accountability. Regularly scheduled ethics workshops ensure that character development is an ongoing emphasis, continually reinforcing the importance of ethical behavior in everyday actions.

Mentorship Programs

Establish mentorship programs that pair less experienced employees with seasoned mentors who exemplify strong character. Mentorship programs provide invaluable support and guidance for employees navigating their personal and professional development. By pairing less experienced employees with mentors who demonstrate exemplary character traits, organizations create opportunities for learning and growth through example. Mentors can offer advice, share experiences, and provide feedback, helping mentees develop their own strong character traits. This one-on-one relationship fosters a culture of continuous improvement and personal growth, ensuring that values such as integrity, empathy, and resilience are passed down and reinforced throughout the organization.

Feedback Mechanisms

Create channels for employees to provide feedback on anything that includes but is not limited to organizational culture and character development initiatives. Effective feedback mechanisms are essential for understanding the impact of programs, projects, and processes, and identifying areas for improvement. Organizations should establish anonymous surveys, suggestion boxes, and regular feedback sessions where employees can share their thoughts and experiences. This feedback helps leadership understand the effectiveness of current initiatives and make necessary adjustments to better support growth. Transparent and open communication channels also strengthen a sense of trust and engagement among employees, encouraging them to actively participate in the organization's character development journey.

Recognition and Rewards

Develop recognition and reward systems that honor employees who consistently demonstrate strong character traits. Recognition and rewards are powerful motivators for reinforcing desired behaviors. Organizations should create programs that acknowledge and celebrate employees who consistently exhibit strong character traits such as integrity, teamwork, and perseverance. This can include formal awards, public recognition, and tangible rewards such as bonuses or additional time off. By highlighting and rewarding ethical behavior, organizations send a clear message that character is valued and essential to the company's success. Recognition programs not only motivate individuals to continue their personal growth but also inspire others to emulate these positive behaviors, contributing to a culture of integrity and excellence.

A strong emphasis on character development leads to a more cohesive, motivated, and ethically driven workforce, ultimately resulting in better organizational performance and a positive reputation. Profits are boosted, as well.

Building strong character traits is a lifelong journey that requires dedication, perseverance, and continuous attention. While challenges are inevitable, adopting effective strategies and creating supportive environments can help individuals stay committed to their goals. Individuals can achieve personal growth and professional success by prioritizing character development and cultivating positive, meaningful relationships. Embracing character development not only enhances individual well-being but also contributes to a more ethical, empathetic, and resilient society.

The story below also shows us how a leader's openness to adopting *The Character Blueprint* can quickly produce results. The *Character Challenge* questions that follow can help us evaluate our own opportunities to improve.

Leadership Scenario: The Promotions Dilemma

After nearly a decade of loyal service, Marcus was promoted to a senior leadership role in a fast-paced tech company. The transition was rocky. Though competent, Marcus began making decisions with little input from his team, prioritizing results over relationships. Turnover numbers crept up.

A peer mentor invited Marcus to a feedback circle—a company practice emphasizing reflection and growth. During the session, Marcus realized he'd stopped seeking input because he feared appearing weak. That day marked a turning point, as he decided to lay ego aside and make changes for everyone's benefit.

Marcus first restructured his one-on-one meetings to include character check-ins. He found employees were surprisingly coachable and willing to learn when he started by asking them to share their honest thoughts and perspectives, showing genuine interest in what they had to say, and expressing his appreciation for their feedback. Only then, did he talk about the character topic of the day. In six months, employee retention stabilized, and morale surged.

"I thought authority meant control," Marcus later admitted. "Now I know it means alignment—with values, with people, and with purpose."

Character Challenge

1. Where in your leadership journey have you seen character emphasis take a back seat to performance focus? How would you have done it differently?

2. What systems (like feedback circles or mentoring) can help sustain character when pressure mounts? Why do you think they help?

3. How can you reinforce values during everyday conversations or decisions with your team?

While the lessons of experience often speak loudest, the evolving workplace demands we keep our eyes open for moments of learning that challenge our assumptions real-time. We are surrounded by opportunities. They exist, if only we choose to see.

Insights From an Old Salt

In this edition of *Insights from an Old Salt*, I would like to share an experience from someone close to me.

When I first joined the company, I wasn't entirely sure what to expect. I'd heard a lot about the organization's commitment to personal growth and fostering a healthy work environment, but I was skeptical. My previous job had been all about results—hit the numbers, and nothing else mattered. There was little regard for how people felt or whether they were developing personally or professionally. I was burnt out and, frankly, a bit cynical about corporate culture.

But from day one at this new company, things felt different. During my onboarding, I was paired with a mentor—not just to show me the ropes but to help me understand the company's values and how they applied to my personal and professional growth. My mentor encouraged me to reflect on my strengths and weaknesses, not as something to fix in isolation but as a foundation for growth. For the first time, I was encouraged to be genuinely introspective at work.

The company also placed a strong emphasis on integrity and accountability. There was a culture of transparency that I hadn't experienced before. Mistakes weren't hidden or punished harshly; instead, they were discussed openly, and the focus was on learning from them. It was liberating to know that I could take risks, speak my mind, and even fail, all without fear of retribution. Over time, I found myself becoming more honest with myself and others, owning my mistakes, and actively working to improve.

Empathy was another cornerstone of the workplace. Leaders modeled this by genuinely listening to concerns and providing support when needed. I remember a time when I was struggling with a project, and instead of the usual pressure to "just get it done," my manager took the time to understand my challenges. We worked together to find a solution, and I was given the space to learn and grow from the experience. It wasn't just about getting the job done but about how I grew through the process.

The environment promoted resilience and adaptability as well. Change was constant, but instead of being a source of stress, it became an opportunity for growth. The company encouraged us to see challenges as chances to develop new skills and perspectives. I noticed that my ability to handle stress improved, and I became more confident in navigating uncertainty.

As I grew personally, I started to notice how these principles impacted the team and the organization. The environment wasn't just about individual character growth—it extended to the way teams functioned and how the organization operated.

Our team meetings became spaces where everyone felt safe to share their ideas, even if they were unconventional. There was a culture of psychological safety that I hadn't experienced before. People weren't afraid to speak up, which led to more innovation and better problem-solving. We knew that our voices mattered, and that made us more engaged and committed to our work.

Work-life balance was also taken seriously. I realized this wasn't just a perk; it was integral to our productivity and well-being. Flexibility was built into the way we worked, and it was clear that the organization valued us as whole people, not just as employees. This respect for our time and well-being made us more motivated and loyal to the company. We were all working hard, but we were also given the space to recharge and take care of our personal lives.

Recognition and appreciation were embedded in our daily routines. Achievements, both big and small, were celebrated. This wasn't just about awards or bonuses, though those were nice, too. It was the small, everyday acknowledgments that made a difference. A simple thank you from a colleague or a shout-out in a meeting went a long way in building a positive atmosphere. It wasn't just about the work we did; it was about how we supported each other in doing it.

Diversity and inclusion weren't just buzzwords—they were reflected in the way we worked together. I could see how different perspectives were valued and how everyone had a seat at the table. It wasn't just about filling quotas; it was about creating a culture where everyone felt they belonged and could contribute. This inclusivity made our teams stronger because we could draw from a wide range of experiences and ideas.

As these principles took root across the organization, I noticed a ripple effect. Our success wasn't just in hitting targets; it was in how we achieved them. The company began to attract more top talent because people wanted to be part of a place where they could grow and thrive. Our reputation in the industry improved, not just for our products and services, but for how we treated our people. There was a sense of pride in being part of something bigger than us, something that was making a positive impact on everyone involved.

Looking back, I can see how this environment has transformed me—not just as an employee, but as a person. I've become more self-aware, resilient, and empathetic. I'm not just focused on what I can achieve but on how I can grow and help others grow along the way. This company has shown me that work doesn't have to be a grind; it can be a place where you become the best version of yourself.

And it's not just me. The impact is visible across the organization. Teams are more cohesive, innovative, and efficient. There's a shared commitment to continuous improvement and a genuine care for each other's well-being. We're not just colleagues; we're a community.

This experience has made me realize that when an organization commits to character development and cultivating a healthy work environment, the benefits are profound and far-reaching. It's not just about building a successful business—it's about creating a place where people can truly thrive, both personally and professionally. And that's a journey worth continuing.

As I reflect, it becomes clear that the true value of work lies not just in the results we produce, but in the experiences we share and the growth we tend within ourselves and others. The lessons I've learned here have changed the way I approach my career, my interactions with colleagues, and even my outlook on life. I've come to understand that a healthy work environment is more than just a nice-to-have—it's essential for both individual and organizational success.

The transformation I've witnessed, both in myself and across the company, is a testament to what's possible when we prioritize character development and a positive work culture. We are all better for it—more engaged, more resilient, and more fulfilled. The sense of purpose and belonging that has emerged is something that I hadn't thought possible in a corporate setting, but it's now the standard by which I measure my professional life.

As we continue this journey together, I encourage each of you to reflect on how you can contribute to your culture, not just for your own benefit but for the collective good. It's a call to action for all of us to take ownership of our growth, support one another, and embrace the principles that have made transformation possible.

In a world where work often feels like a race against time, I've learned that slowing down to focus on character and connection can lead to outcomes far beyond what we might have imagined. It's about building a legacy—not just of success, but of significance. And that is something truly worth striving for.

So, as we move forward, let's continue to nurture this environment, celebrate our collective progress, and remain committed to creating a workplace where everyone can flourish. After all, the work we do is important, but the way we do it—and the people we become along the way—is what truly matters.

Chapter 12: A Call to Action

Creating healthy work environments through individual character development and fostering highly efficient teams is a profound and transformative endeavor. As we conclude this book, it is essential to reflect on the insights and strategies we have explored and translate them into actionable steps. This final chapter serves as a call to action, urging leaders and team members alike to take concrete strides toward elevating environments where people prosper, teams excel, and organizations achieve sustainable success.

1. Lead by Example

Leadership is not about titles, positions, or power—it's about influence and setting a standard of behavior that others can look up to. The most powerful and sustainable change starts with individuals who are committed to leading by example. For any transformation to take root, leaders must first embody the traits they wish to see in their teams. As a leader, everything you do, from how you make decisions to how you treat others, will be observed and often replicated by those around you. Your actions are a megaphone speaking at a volume no words or organizational policies could ever match.

If you want to create a culture of integrity, leaders must first model integrity in every decision, even when it's hard. For example, when faced with an opportunity to shade the truth for immediate gain—whether it's overstating a team's achievements or downplaying an issue to avoid accountability—you must stand firm in your commitment to honesty. Transparency is key. Character-committed leaders admit mistakes when they happen and use them as teachable moments rather than trying to cover them up. A leader who owns their imperfections sets a powerful precedent proving errors are simply fertilizer that feeds growth and not a reflection of weakness.

Moreover, leading by example embodies more than concentrating on positive behaviors, it also actively addresses negative ones. If an environment of unwavering respect for all is important to you, you cannot afford to stay silent when you see instances of exclusion or disrespect. Speak up, even when it's uncomfortable, and make it clear that unethical behavior, no matter how it's expressed, won't be tolerated. Leading by example also means being accessible. Take the time to engage with your team members, understand their challenges, and demonstrate empathy and support. A sense of belonging and trust motivates individuals to give their best.

2. Foster Open Communication

A culture of open communication is the backbone of any healthy and high-performing team. Without it, misunderstandings, resentment, and inefficiencies quickly emerge, leading to a toxic work environment. True open communication means creating a space where individuals feel safe to share their ideas, feedback, and concerns without fear of retaliation or judgment. It requires transparency from top to bottom and bottom to top.

The first step in fostering open communication is to establish psychological safety. This means that team members must feel comfortable expressing dissenting opinions or pointing out issues without worrying about negative consequences. For example, an employee who notices a flaw in a project plan should feel empowered to raise the issue, knowing that their concern will be taken seriously rather than dismissed as insubordination. As a leader, you can encourage this by actively soliciting input from all levels of the organization. Regularly ask your team for feedback, and more importantly, take action, even if you cannot do exactly what the employee requests or suggests. Simply communicate the "what" and "why" behind those decisions. When employees see implementations of their suggestions, or receive the respect of a commonsense explanation for why a change wasn't made, it reinforces the idea that their voices matter.

Another aspect of open communication requires yet another layer of transparency from leadership. This doesn't mean oversharing confidential information, but it does mean keeping your team informed about important decisions, goals, and changes. When teams are kept in the dark, rumors and uncertainty can spread, which undermines trust and confidence. Regular updates, whether through meetings, newsletters, or town halls, help ensure that everyone is aligned and working toward the same objectives.

Listening is equally important in fostering open communication. Leaders often make the mistake of assuming they know what's going on within their teams, but without truly listening to employees, they miss critical insights. Practicing active listening—where you fully concentrate, understand, and respond to what is being said—demonstrates respect for the speaker and can uncover hidden challenges or opportunities that otherwise might have been missed.

Some employees may feel hesitant to speak up in group settings, so offering various ways to communicate privately, can provide additional comfort for those of an introverted nature. This ensures that no valuable input is left unheard.

Open communication requires vigilance, regular check-ins, and, most importantly, the willingness to act on what is being shared. It's not enough to simply say, "My door is always open." Leaders must actively demonstrate that they are not only willing to listen but eager to engage.

3. Invest in Personal and Team Development

In today's competitive and rapidly changing work environment, an organization that does not invest in the continuous development of its people is one that risks stagnation. Personal and team development is not a luxury; it is a necessity for both individual growth and overall organizational success. While many organizations understand the importance of technical training, fewer place the same emphasis on character development, which is equally essential for building resilient, collaborative, and high-performing teams.

Personal development begins with self-awareness. Encourage individuals to reflect on their strengths, weaknesses, and areas for growth. This can be facilitated through tools such as comprehensive assessments, educational forums, or coaching sessions. Providing employees with opportunities to understand their own emotional intelligence, how they relate to others, and how they handle stress—can be transformative. When individuals have a clear understanding of who they are, why they react or respond like they do, and how they operate within a team, they can better contribute to the progress of the organization.

Team development is equally crucial. High-performing teams are not created by chance; they are built through intentional development and collaboration. This involves more than just team-building exercises. Regular workshops on identifying corporate weaknesses, conflict resolution, collaboration, communication, and even loss prevention can help teams develop the skills they need to navigate challenges effectively. Leaders should also encourage cross-functional collaboration to ensure that teams are not working in silos. Cross-team projects and knowledge-sharing initiatives help build a more unified, innovative organization.

Mentorship and coaching programs can significantly enhance both personal and team development. Pairing less experienced employees with seasoned mentors not only accelerates individual growth but also instills a sense of community and knowledge transfer within the organization. Mentors can guide individuals through challenges, help them navigate organizational dynamics, and provide career advice that strengthens their professional trajectory. Leaders should also consider investing in external coaches who can provide specialized guidance on leadership development, team dynamics, and emotional intelligence.

Furthermore, career development pathways are essential if you want to retain top talent. Employees who see a clear path for growth within an organization are more likely to stay engaged and motivated. Outlining opportunities for advancement, whether through promotions, lateral moves, or leadership training, shows a commitment to an employee's long-term success.

Investing in personal and team development ensures a return in the future of the organization. When individuals feel that their growth is a priority, they are more likely to bring their best selves to work, contributing at the highest levels.

4. Prioritize Well-being

In today's fast-paced and often high-pressured work environments, prioritizing employee well-being has shifted from being a "nice-to-have" to an absolute necessity. The mental, physical, and emotional health of individuals directly impacts their performance, engagement, and long-term sustainability within an organization. Leaders who genuinely prioritize the well-being of their team members create an environment where people feel appreciated, supported, and motivated to perform at their best without the risk of burnout.

The first step in prioritizing well-being is recognizing that it is multifaceted. Physical health is just one aspect; mental and emotional health are equally important and often overlooked. Workplaces should actively establish an environment where employees feel comfortable discussing their mental health and accessing the resources they need. This can include offering employee assistance programs (EAPs) that provide confidential counseling, mental health days, and promoting a culture where taking time off for mental well-being is normalized, not stigmatized. Leaders should regularly remind employees of these resources and set the example by using them when needed. The message should be clear: emotional well-being is a priority, not an afterthought.

Work-life balance is another critical aspect of well-being. The era of "always-on" work culture, where employees are expected to respond to emails at all hours, is unsustainable and leads to chronic stress. Leaders can combat this by setting clear boundaries around work hours and respecting time off. Encouraging flexible work arrangements, whether through remote work options or adaptable hours, can give employees the autonomy they need to manage both their professional and personal responsibilities. However, flexibility must come with trust; employees should not feel micromanaged or judged based on the hours they work, but rather on the quality of their contributions.

Physical well-being should also be considered. This can range from providing healthy snacks in the office to offering gym memberships or on-site fitness classes. Some companies have embraced "walking meetings" or stretching breaks to encourage physical activity throughout the day. Additionally, ergonomics should be prioritized to ensure that workspaces are conducive to long-term physical health, preventing injuries from repetitive strain or poor posture. A side-benefit of improved ergonomics is the high statistical probability of greater efficiency, which leads to better profits.

A culture of well-being also results in leaders who model healthy behaviors. If leadership is seen working late every night, skipping vacations, and glorifying overwork, employees will feel pressured to follow suit. Instead, leaders should demonstrate a balanced approach to work by taking regular breaks, setting boundaries for themselves, and practicing mindfulness or stress-relief techniques. When leaders show that they value their own health, it sends a powerful message to the rest of the organization about the importance of balance.

Prioritizing well-being is not just about avoiding burnout—it's about promoting an environment where people can perform at their best in a sustainable way. When employees feel supported in their physical, mental, and emotional health, they are more engaged, productive, and loyal.

5. Cultivate Accountability and Ownership

Accountability is the bedrock of any high-performing team. It ensures that every member is responsible for their actions, decisions, and the outcomes of their work. When accountability is embedded into the culture of an organization, it empowers individuals to take ownership of their responsibilities and undergirds a sense of trust and respect among team members. Accountability requires more than simply setting clear expectations—it consists of systems, communication, and leadership that align with these values.

The first step in building accountability is clarity. Every team member should know exactly what is expected of them, both in terms of tasks and behavior. Leaders must be clear about goals, deadlines, and the standards by which success is measured. Vague or inconsistent expectations lead to confusion and excuses. When goals and responsibilities are straightforward, individuals have a concrete understanding of what they need to deliver and by when, which minimizes the risk of blame-shifting or procrastination.

Accountability must also be reciprocal. While leaders should expect accountability from their team members, they must also hold themselves accountable. This means owning up to mistakes when they happen and being transparent about decisions that affect the team and the reasons behind them. When leaders take responsibility for their actions, it sets the tone for everyone, demonstrating that accountability is a value that applies to all, not just for those at the bottom of the hierarchy.

Creating an environment of trust is essential for accountability to advance. Team members must feel that they can rely on each other to follow through on their commitments. Trust-building comes from consistent communication and follow-through on promises. If one team member consistently misses deadlines or delivers subpar work without any consequences, it erodes confidence and damages morale. Leaders must be vigilant in addressing these issues swiftly and constructively, providing support and feedback to improve performance where needed.

To further strengthen accountability, encourage autonomy within the team. When individuals are given the freedom to make decisions about how they complete their work, they are more likely to feel a sense of ownership over their outcomes. Micromanagement, on the other hand, diminishes accountability by taking away personal responsibility. Leaders should focus on outcomes rather than dictating every step an employee takes in a the process. A leader following *The Character Blueprint* trusts that their team members have the skills and knowledge to achieve the desired results. They hold their people accountable, when necessary, without holding their thumbs on them, otherwise.

Accountability is not about punishing failure; it's about creating a framework where individuals can honestly talk and seek support when needed. If mistakes are made, they are viewed as learning opportunities, with an emphasis on growth rather than blame. Regular check-ins and reviews provide opportunities to discuss progress, address any challenges, and recalibrate expectations if necessary.

6. Embrace Diversity and Include

Diversity and inclusion are not just buzzwords—they are essential components of a thriving, innovative, and resilient organization. Diverse teams bring together a wide range of perspectives, experiences, and skills that can lead to more creative problem-solving and better decision-making. However, diversity alone is not enough; inclusion ensures that every individual, regardless of their background, feels valued, respected, and able to contribute fully to the team. To create truly inclusive work environments, leaders must take intentional, sustained actions.

The first step in embracing diversity is recognizing its value. Research consistently shows that diverse teams outperform homogenous ones, especially in complex, creative, or problem-solving tasks. Leaders should actively seek to build teams that include a wide range of experiences, viewpoints, and cultural backgrounds. This may involve rethinking hiring practices to ensure that job postings, interview processes, and promotion criteria are free from unconscious bias. Consider forming partnerships with organizations that support underrepresented groups, ensuring that your talent pipeline includes diverse candidates from all walks of life.

Inclusion, however, goes beyond simply having diverse representation on your team. It's about creating an environment where all individuals feel they belong and can contribute without fear of judgment or exclusion. Leaders must be proactive in addressing the subtle dynamics that can create barriers to inclusion. For instance, if certain voices dominate meetings while others remain silent, it is the leader's responsibility to facilitate balanced participation. Encouraging every team member to contribute their ideas ensures that all perspectives are heard.

It's also important to understand that inclusion is not a one-size-fits-all approach. Everyone has unique needs and preferences when it comes to feeling included. This is where empathy and emotional intelligence play a crucial role. Leaders should take the time to get to know their team members on a personal level, understanding their communication styles, strengths, and any challenges they might face. For example, introverted team members may prefer sharing their ideas in writing, while others may thrive in group discussions. Adapting your leadership style to meet these diverse needs shows a commitment to true inclusion.

Creating an inclusive culture also means addressing systemic barriers that may exist within the organization. Conduct regular audits of policies, practices, and company culture to identify any areas where certain groups may be disadvantaged. This could include looking at promotion rates, pay equity, or opportunities for professional development. Taking action to correct these imbalances ensures that everyone has an equal opportunity to succeed.

Finally, inclusion must be celebrated. Recognizing and valuing diversity should be woven into the fabric of your organization. This can be achieved through diversity training programs, celebrating cultural differences, and creating employee resource groups (ERGs) that provide a safe space for underrepresented groups to connect and support each other. When individuals feel that their unique identities are acknowledged and celebrated, they are more likely to bring their full selves to work, leading to greater engagement and innovation.

Diversity and inclusion are not optional; they are essential for creating a dynamic, forward-thinking organization. By fostering an environment where everyone feels they belong and can contribute their unique strengths, leaders set the stage for teams that are more innovative, resilient, and capable of solving the complex challenges of today's business world.

7. Measure and Celebrate Success

To drive sustained success, it's critical to regularly measure progress and celebrate achievements. While many organizations are adept at calculating tangible outcomes like revenue, project completions, or customer satisfaction, fewer put the same effort into evaluating how well they are acting on their values and supporting character-driven success. Creating metrics for character development, team dynamics, and personal growth can provide invaluable insight into how well your organization is thriving beyond the bottom line.

Start by defining what success looks like in terms of character. For example, if integrity is a core value, how is it being demonstrated across different levels of the organization? Are there systems in place to track ethical decision-making or examples of individuals standing up for what's right? Implement regular reviews, where individuals receive feedback from peers, subordinates, and supervisors. This can highlight strengths and areas for development related to character traits such as empathy, leadership, and resilience. Remember, for this phase, your goal is not to catch things done wrong, but instead, to recognize measurable outcomes from victories big and small.

It's also essential to celebrate both individual and team successes. Recognition boosts morale and reinforces the behaviors you want to see more of within your organization. However, celebrating success goes beyond financial rewards or public recognition; it's about acknowledging the effort and growth that led to the achievement. For instance, if a team navigated a difficult project while upholding values like respect and collaboration, highlight how those values contributed to the outcome. This not only reinforces the importance of character but also motivates others to follow suit.

Celebrating small wins along the way can also keep momentum going, especially during long-term projects. Acknowledging progress, even if the final goal hasn't been reached, helps maintain motivation and engagement. This could be done through team shout-outs, personal notes from leadership, or informal recognition events that highlight individual contributions.

Success should be a shared experience. Foster a culture where team members celebrate each other's achievements rather than viewing success as a zero-sum game. By promoting a spirit of collective accomplishment, you build stronger teams that are more invested in each other's growth and success.

Creating thriving work environments rooted in strong character is a long-term adventure that requires intentional leadership, open communication, investment in development, a commitment to well-being, accountability, inclusion, and continuous measurement. Leaders and team members alike must embrace this blueprint as a living, evolving process. By doing so, we can create more workplaces where people, teams, and organizations not only succeed but also flourish—creating lasting, positive impact.

Every action step we've covered should be a regular undertaking for leaders committed to *The Character Blueprint.* But for those moments when you need a quick-hit reminder, I've put together an easy-to-follow priority list.

Character Leadership Toolkit

5 Daily Practices to Help You Lead with Character:

1. **Morning Check-In:** Ask yourself, *What do I stand for today?*

2. **Pause for Perspective:** Take a breath before reacting—especially under stress.

3. **Inclusive Leadership:** Notice who isn't speaking. Invite their voice.

4. **Model Vulnerability:** Share a mistake and what it taught you.

5. **End-of-Day Reflection:** *Did I lead with empathy and integrity today?*

Now is the time to act. The foundation has been laid; the strategies are in place. It's up to each of us, in our own roles, to put these principles into practice and build the kind of workplaces that inspire greatness in everyone involved.

The Legacy of Character-Driven Leadership

As we move from theory into practice, it's essential to understand the lasting impact of character-driven leadership. This type of leadership not only creates immediate results, it also leaves a legacy that transforms organizational culture over time. When character becomes the foundation of leadership, it shapes the future in profound and enduring ways.

Character-driven leaders understand that success is not merely about achieving targets but about building sustainable systems, relationships, and cultures that can weather both internal and external challenges. Organizations led by such leaders are better equipped to adapt to changing market conditions, global disruptions, and the evolving needs of their employees. When challenges arise, these leaders don't panic or look for shortcuts; they trust the foundation they've built and use it as a springboard for thoughtful, courageous decision-making.

One of the most significant legacies a leader can leave behind is the development of other leaders. Character-driven leadership isn't about holding onto power but about empowering others to step into their own leadership potential. Leaders who model strong character traits—integrity, empathy, honesty, humility, resilience—set an example for others to follow. They inspire those around them to adopt the same values, fostering a cycle of growth and development that extends far beyond their tenure. This ensures that the organization continues to thrive long after they've moved on to new roles or responsibilities.

Moreover, character-driven leaders create a ripple effect that extends beyond the organization's walls. Their approach to leadership influences not just the workplace but also the communities, families, and networks connected to the organization. Employees who experience respect, inclusion, and empowerment at work carry those values into their personal lives, strengthening relationships and contributing positively where they live.

A Sustainable Future: The Role of Organizations

As organizations, we have a crucial role in ensuring that character development and ethical leadership are not just encouraged but embedded in the very fabric of how we operate. Building a sustainable future means creating systems, policies, and environments that not only support but demand a commitment to *The Character Blueprint*. The pursuit of profit should never come at the expense of foundational principles, because ultimately, the true measure of success lies in how an organization treats its people and contributes to society.

Sustainability, in this context, refers to more than just long-term business survival or environmental responsibility. It encompasses the idea of building businesses that last, through ethical practices, strong leadership, and a commitment to long-term value creation over short-term gains. Organizations that prioritize character not only attract top talent but also cultivate loyalty, trust, and engagement. These are the pillars of sustainability in a modern economy where employees and consumers alike are increasingly driven by purpose, values, and a desire to be part of something bigger than themselves.

Organizations also need to be transparent in their commitment to character and sustainability. This means holding themselves accountable not just to shareholders but also to employees, customers, and society at large. Reporting on initiatives related to employee well-being, environmental impact, and community influence should be as important as financial reporting. Transparency builds trust, and trust is the currency of sustainable organizations.

Your Next Steps: Bringing the Blueprint to Life

Now that you've explored the principles and strategies outlined in this book, it's time to take the next step—bringing these concepts to life within your own organization, team, or personal leadership journey. Change doesn't happen overnight, and transforming workplace culture or personal behavior takes time, effort, and commitment. But with a clear plan and a willingness to lead by example, you can begin to implement *The Character Blueprint* in meaningful ways.

Start by reflecting on your own leadership endeavors. Ask yourself:

- Where do I excel in terms of character?
- Where do I need to grow?

Being honest with yourself about your strengths and areas for improvement is the first step to becoming a more effective, character-driven leader. Consider seeking feedback from those around you—colleagues, team members, or mentors—to gain a broader perspective on how your leadership is perceived and where you can improve.

Next, identify one or two areas where you can begin to implement change immediately. This might involve creating opportunities for open communication within your team, prioritizing well-being by encouraging work-life balance, or taking steps to include those who have been silenced in your workplace. Small, consistent changes can make a significant impact over time, especially when they are rooted in a commitment to strong values.

It's also essential to build a support system. Whether through mentorship, peer groups, coaching, or leadership training, surrounding yourself with others who are committed to character-driven leadership can help keep you accountable and inspired. Leadership can be a lonely road, but you don't have to walk it alone. Seek out those who challenge and support you, and who are equally dedicated to fostering ethical and thriving workplaces.

As you implement these changes, remember to celebrate progress. Acknowledge the wins, both big and small, and recognize the people who are contributing to positive change within your organization. Success is a life-long adventure, not a final destination, and it's important to celebrate each step along the way.

Lastly, keep the vision of a character-driven workplace at the forefront of everything you do. Let it guide your decisions, inspire your leadership, and serve as a reminder of the lasting impact you can have on others. As a leader, your influence is powerful—use it to build workplaces where people feel empowered to bring their best selves to work, where teams are united by shared values, and where success is defined not only by what is achieved, but by how it is accomplished.

Reflection Challenge: Craft Your Character Leadership Statement

Think about the leader you admire most. What makes them unforgettable? Now turn inward.

Write your own Character Leadership Statement.

- What do you want to be remembered for?
- Which values drive your decisions?
- How will you keep growing when no one is watching?

Example Statement:

I lead with empathy, consistency, and courage. I will speak for those not in the room, listen more than I speak, and hold myself accountable when I miss the mark.

The Legacy of Character

As we close, I want to offer one final reminder that the blueprint you build today can shape not just your leadership—but your legacy. Character-driven leadership has the potential to change not just individual lives but entire organizations and industries. It is essential in today's complex, interconnected world.

The journey begins with you. Whether you are a seasoned leader, a team member, or an emerging professional, you have the power to make a difference by committing to character in your daily actions. By doing so, you will contribute to a legacy of ethical leadership that will inspire future generations.

This is your call to action: Embrace the blueprint, live your values, and lead with character. In doing so, you will help build the kind of workplaces where people flourish, teams excel, and lasting success is achieved. The world needs leaders who are not only skilled but principled. Who understand that true success is about more than just outcomes; it's about making a positive, lasting impact on those around them. Be that leader.

Our future is in your hands. Make it one of integrity, purpose, and character. *The Character Blueprint* was designed with you in mind.

Call to Action:
Choose to Make a
Difference

Made in the USA
Columbia, SC
11 June 2025

59169353R00100